Pokeweed and Mrs. Gasp

A Lillenas DRAMA RESOURCE

POKEWEED AND MRS. GASP

And Other One-Acts with a Point of View

by Anita Higman

Cover art: Paul Franitza

Printed in the United States of America

To my
husband and friend,
Peter.
Thank you for your encouragement,
your love,
and the marvelous way you pretend
to like my tofu stroganoff.

drama
is the
fertile field
given by His sovereign hand
to nourish
and harvest imaginings
for a feast
to celebrate
His plan.

Anita Higman

Contents

Breaking Ground

I toyed with the idea of opening this introductory piece with a hopelessly peacockery sounding analogy about playwriting. Something like, "It's intriguing to note that the process of writing drama possesses a somewhat congruent relationship to other art forms, such as painting a picture. Many of the substantive components of both creative forms are shared. For instance, there is the need for correct perspective, the precise yet ethereal blending of lights and darks, and that infinitely fascinating quality of lifelikeness."

Then I changed my mind.

I will break ground with this down-to-earth comment instead. Playwriting is sometimes like eating a chocolate mousse and sometimes like the nerve-jangling scrape of fork prongs across a glass plate.

But when the final tally is taken, playwriting definitely flies to a higher nest for me than novel writing. The reason for this is that I have a dinosaur-sized, terror-breathing fear of creating narrative.

So, some years ago I tucked my stories away, with all their befuddling verbiage about the landscape, and began to cultivate my fascination for intoxicating banter. (You know, the kinds of delicious things we only dream of saying, because our perfect response always comes when the other person is five miles down the road.)

When I'm not ferreting out characters and their dialogue from my cerebral hemispheres, I'm spending the evening in unbridled bliss reading the dictionary. (Actually, that is how I found the titles for two of my plays.)

So, if you will please excuse me now, I have another madcap evening planned with Mr. Webster.

Anita Higman
Houston

The Eclipse of Mr. Cole

Cast of Characters

ERNEST COLE: Ernest Cole is an account executive for Hastings Advertising Agency, Inc. He is single and can be either in his 20s or 30s. Ernest is witty, intelligent, and creative. Even though he is very skeptical about Christianity, deep in his heart he wants to find the peace that has always been missing in his life.

LILLY: Lilly is also an account executive for Hastings Advertising Agency, Inc. She is single and can be either in her 20s or 30s. Lilly has a sense of humor and loves her work. She is a Christian and exudes an inner peace and joy that is very appealing in her character.

TOM: Tom is also an account executive at Hastings. He can be either in his 20s or 30s. Tom is somewhat self-centered and rather unenterprising at his job.

Scene

We are inside the basement of a small mansion in a large American city. The mansion has been remodeled into office space for Hastings Advertising Agency. An old file cabinet sits left center, one old crate sits right center, and another crate sits next to the file cabinet. Miscellaneous stacks of paper and other office debris are on the floor of the basement. The time is noon on a workday in the present.

Props

General:	Old file cabinet
	Two old crates
	Stacks of paper and office debris (optional)
LILLY:	Lunch bag
	Sandwich wrapped in foil
	Two square cookies
ERNEST:	Briefcase
	Four pencils
	Watch

At Rise

Ernest is sitting on the basement floor center stage. He is wearing formal business attire, except for his wild-colored tie. His suit coat is draped neatly across his briefcase, and his sleeves are rolled up. He is fiddling with four pencils in his hand.

(LILLY *enters through the basement door, stage left.* LILLY *is dressed in an attractive business outfit and is carrying her lunch bag.* ERNEST *remains on the floor, watching her.)*

ERNEST: You look guilty of something.

LILLY *(gasps and spins around to see who is speaking):* Ernest. You startled me. What in the world are you doing down here in the basement?

ERNEST: I'm communing with this cockroach on the floor. We're meditating upon our oneness in the cosmic universe.

LILLY *(jokingly):* Aren't you supposed to have some crystals to do that with?

ERNEST: You must be *into* New Age.

LILLY: I would be if I thought I was God.

ERNEST: I don't take anything too seriously, really . . . except for making money.

LILLY: Sounds as dangerous as New Age.

ERNEST: Oh, but a little danger is a small price to pay for the immeasurable glories of wealth. *(Pause)* You never did say what brings *you* down here to the basement.

LILLY *(sits down on a crate):* I come down here sometimes to eat my lunch and sometimes to . . . pray.

ERNEST: Pray? Well, what sort of praying do you do? Let's see, there's the Buddhism stuff . . . the Hinduism and Confucianism stuff . . . the . . . am I getting warm?

LILLY: Nope.

ERNEST: Oh, no. It's not the Christianity stuff, is it?

LILLY: Well, I am a Christian, but you make it sound like a disease.

ERNEST: It is. I remember catching it once in Sunday School when I was a kid.

LILLY: Sounds like you didn't like Sunday School very much.

ERNEST: Oh, it was all right, I guess. But my father didn't approve of my going, so I quit. He said I'd just fill my head with spiritual nerve gas . . . then I'd never be good for anything in the real world. "There isn't a hard thing in this life," he used to say, "that can't be tenderized with the mallets of hard cash and hard liquor."

LILLY: And is that what *you* think?

ERNEST: Who knows? *(Looks at* LILLY*'s lunch bag)* So, what are you having for lunch there . . . goose pâté on a croissant?

LILLY *(unwraps her sandwich and holds it up):* Tofu on whole wheat. Would you like half?

ERNEST: Tofu. Sounds like a fungus that grows in the dark.

LILLY: It's just bean curd.

ERNEST *(lightly):* Oh, boy, that makes me feel a lot better.

LILLY: Would you like half or not?

ERNEST *(while carefully sticking a pencil in each of his ears and one in each nostril, as if performing a great balancing act):* No. Ernest Cole never eats anything that might upset the natural and perfect balance of junk food in his body.

LILLY *(friendly):* You're bizarre. *(Takes a bite of her sandwich)*

ERNEST *(removes pencils):* In the ad business you've got to have a bizarre mind. It's a survival thing . . . like blood to a mosquito and dirt to a worm and bacteria to a . . .

LILLY *(interrupting):* Do you think you could put a leash on those metaphors during lunch, please?

ERNEST: Sorry.

LILLY: I was just wondering about something. I don't hear the name Ernest much anymore. Did your mother name you after someone in your family?

ERNEST: Who knows?

LILLY: Maybe she thought like my mother, that maybe at some point in our lives we'd need moral encouragement.

ERNEST: Why would you say something like that?

LILLY: Would you like a health-nut cookie?

ERNEST: You are deliberately changing the subject. *(Pause)* You know, I still think that's unusual, you coming down here to eat and pray.

LILLY: Well, it's not as strange as coming down here to have a religious experience with an insect. *(Holding up a square cookie)* Are you sure you don't want one? I made them myself.

ERNEST *(accepting the cookie from* LILLY*)*: OK. Thanks. *(Takes bite of cookie and has a hard time chewing it)*

LILLY: How's the cookie?

ERNEST: Well, if you don't mind the spinach flavor and tree bark texture, they're quite good.

LILLY: Listen . . . I have something important I need to talk to you about, and this seems like maybe a good time.

ERNEST: Let me guess. You need some brainstorming with old Ernest for that dog deodorant commercial. Right?

LILLY: No. That's going fine. It's something else.

ERNEST: Sounds serious.

LILLY: It is.

ERNEST: Well . . . what is it?

LILLY *(seriously)*: I know what's been going on around here, Ernest.

ERNEST: Whooo. Sounds like a good mystery.

LILLY: It isn't, because I know whodunit.

ERNEST: OK, I confess. I wasn't really communing with that cockroach over there. I just squashed him, and it wasn't even in self-defense.

LILLY: I can't discuss this with you if everything is to be a joke.

ERNEST: All right. Go ahead.

LILLY: I know . . . that you have been systematically cheating the company out of money for months.

ERNEST: Now who's joking.

LILLY: Is that all you have to say?

ERNEST: On that subject, yes.

LILLY: Well, I was hoping you would go ahead and confess.

ERNEST: Sorry, but no cigar. *(Pause)* You're serious about this, aren't you?

LILLY: As serious as *you* were when you pilfered the money.

ERNEST: I hope you haven't been spreading this gossip around the office.

LILLY: No. I wanted to talk to *you* about it.

ERNEST: What proof do you have anyway? Just some wild hunch?

LILLY: No, it's more than that. And I think I finally figured out how you did it.

ERNEST: Look, I know this may sound rough, but I'll have the right to sue for defamation of character if you take this information out of this room.

LILLY: But you won't sue me.

ERNEST: And why not?

LILLY: Because you know that what I've said is the absolute truth. I happened to come across some documents of yours.

ERNEST: Documents?

LILLY: That's right. You know the ones I mean. And all of your personal notes were still attached. I'm sure you meant to throw them away, but you didn't.

ERNEST: How dare you go through my locked desk.

LILLY: I didn't. The documents were in my top drawer.

ERNEST: I don't believe you.

LILLY: They were placed in a way that made me think someone wanted me to find them.

ERNEST: Perhaps my assistant is a traitor too. I'll fire her immediately after lunch.

LILLY: But what about me? You can't fire me too.

ERNEST: So what is this? You'll keep quiet if I pay you? I guess the little praying mantis is truly a predator.

LILLY: You've misunderstood. I don't want money.

ERNEST: Then what do you want?

LILLY: Why did you steal from the company?

ERNEST: I didn't take that much. I only dipped my finger in the honey pot.

LILLY: From the figures on those documents, I'd say you *fell* into the honey pot.

ERNEST: I repeat. What do you want?

LILLY: I just wanted you to know that I know. And that I am praying for you to do the right thing.

ERNEST *(laughing)*: Are you serious?

LILLY: Yes.

ERNEST: Dear, sweet Lilly . . . what a strange game you play. It's been quite a lark, but I think I'll pass on the next round.

LILLY: If you think all of this is a game, then you are in more trouble than you think.

ERNEST: You're wrong . . . because I have the genetic code for invincibility. I inherited it from my father.

LILLY: And was your father a thief as well?

ERNEST: We are not really thieves. I like to think of us more as . . . moralistic mavericks.

LILLY: Now I wonder if *you're* serious.

ERNEST: Look at it this way. My adjustments in the company's finances might save them some taxes.

LILLY: Well, perhaps the company will send you a thank-you note while you're in jail.

ERNEST: Oh, but I'm not going to prison.

LILLY: Do you intend to live your whole life this way?

ERNEST: My father always said that in order to get ahead, you had to treat life like a slot machine and people as coins.

LILLY: You keep referring to your father and what *he* said. What do *you* say?

ERNEST: I say his philosophy wasn't without merit.

LILLY: So you have your doubts?

ERNEST: Well, don't you have your doubts about God?

LILLY: That isn't the same.

ERNEST: Why not?

LILLY: Because God is God whether I'm having a moment of weakness or not, but your father is *human* and subject to error.

ERNEST: God is such a foreign concept to me.

LILLY: Is that your father speaking again? (ERNEST *does not answer.)* Your father didn't treat you well, did he?

ERNEST: No matter how my father treated me . . . I always understood him. *(Pause)* Cheat or be cheated. It was a simple philosophy, but it took him from nothing to a position that none of his ancestors could have even dreamed of. And all the people who shook their heads at my father spent the rest of their years trying to shake out his wallet.

LILLY: I'm sorry.

ERNEST: My father lived and died and managed never to let any of them get away with anything . . . including me.

LILLY: I don't know what to say.

ERNEST: You could say that you'll drop this accusation against me.

LILLY: Now *I* feel like a coin in your slot machine.

ERNEST: Perhaps you are.

LILLY: I have one more personal question that I have no right to ask.

ERNEST: All right. One more.

LILLY: Did you embezzle from the company to get back at your father, or was it to try and live up to his expectations?

ERNEST: Hey, who knows anything in this life? Maybe my subconscious just recognizes that money is on a higher plane than people . . . more trustworthy. *(Pause)* Or maybe, I skimmed off that money simply because I needed it.

LILLY: I doubt that, since you probably make a generous salary here.

ERNEST: Look, the people I take from, take from me every day. Every time they cut my benefits while they enjoy skyrocketing profits, they steal from *me.* I'm doing no more than leveling the scales a bit.

LILLY: If you could only hear yourself.

ERNEST: I'm surprised you're not concerned about the imbalance here. They cut your benefits too. Of course, if you ever change your mind, you'll have to find your own entrance into the honey pot.

LILLY: I'm more interested in sleeping well at night.

ERNEST: Who gave you permission to be my conscience? *(Pause)* I know what you want. But if I turn myself in . . . my life and career will go straight down the tubes. *(Pause)* Look, only you and I and my assistant know about this. I'll pay off my assistant to keep her quiet. No one else need know, and I promise you right now that I will not continue this activity. OK? Will that take care of it?

LILLY: You said only three of us know . . . but God knows.

ERNEST: And what is He going to do about it? I can't wait to see how God is going to come down here and get me to turn myself in. *(Pause)* You didn't really come to the basement to eat and pray, did you? It was just to trap what you thought was a skunk and then watch it gnaw its own foot off to save itself.

LILLY: I didn't even know you were down here in the basement.

ERNEST: Maybe you're lying. And maybe you're lying about not telling anyone else too. Lying is a sin, you know.

LILLY: So it's all right for you to steal, but it's not all right for me to lie?

ERNEST: So you admit you've been lying?

LILLY: No. I'm just trying to figure out what kind of ethical game you play.

ERNEST: Let's just drop it, OK?

(TOM *enters through basement door.)*

TOM *(to* ERNEST *and* LILLY): Hello. Excuse me.

LILLY: Hi, Tom. What's up?

ERNEST *(to* TOM): How did you know we were down here?

TOM: Hey, I come down here sometimes. It's the only demilitarized zone in the building. Listen, Ernest, I . . . you . . . I don't know quite how to say this, but . . .

ERNEST: But what?

TOM: Well, Mr. Hastings wants you in his office in exactly 20 minutes.

ERNEST: Me? Why?

TOM: I'm not at liberty to say.

ERNEST: Come on, Tom, this is good ol' Ernest you're talking to. (TOM *remains silent.)* Well, you can at least tell me if it's good or bad.

TOM: It's bad.

ERNEST: How bad?

TOM: You don't want to know.

ERNEST: Humor me.

TOM: If you insist. I heard Mr. Hastings say, "I think I smell the foul winds of human greed, and I think it's coming from the office of Ernest Cole."

ERNEST: Well, you know how he's got a flair for theatrics. It's probably nothing.

TOM: I think it's more than nothing.

ERNEST: Really?

TOM: I know I'm going to hate myself for telling you this, but your assistant, Ms. Gray, has been stirring up some stink for you.

ERNEST: I knew it. *(Pause)* You know, she's been trying to ruin me all along. I overheard her last Friday saying to Martin that she intended to get my job, one way or another.

TOM: That may very well be, but you're still nailed. Ms. Gray has a whole pile of papers, signatures, everything that proves . . . well, I think you know what it proves.

ERNEST: So you know all about everything?

TOM: Most of it.

ERNEST: Maybe this is really an opportunity in disguise. We can now all plead our case to Hastings that he isn't paying us enough. Why, you're always complaining about that, Tom.

TOM: Right, but I'll never do anything about it.

ERNEST: Well, this is *it* then. Your opportunity to shine. To let old Hastings know just how you feel about his mistreatment of all of his employees . . . so much so that one of them has been forced to resort to . . . well, you get my drift.

TOM: Yeah, I do get the drift . . . and I'll bet that drift takes me right over the rapids without a boat.

ERNEST: Well, he likes you. Hastings will do anything you say. Be a friend to me, OK?

TOM: Ernest, you know we've never really been friends.

ERNEST: Yeah, but I really need one now. OK?

TOM: No, it's not OK. How would it look? I can't back you, or they'll assume I was in on it too. I have to think of my job . . . and my family.

ERNEST: Well, maybe Hastings will just give me a pay cut.

TOM: From what I heard, I think your next cut will come from a guillotine.

ERNEST: But this isn't fair! I was chosen Employee of the Year. What about the big luncheon in my honor next week? I deserve my day in the sun.

TOM: Fair is fair. You eclipsed your own day in the sun.

ERNEST: Why are you suddenly witty? In all the months I've worked with you, the ideas you contributed to our team were as provocative as dead weeds. But now, now that I'm clutched in the tentacles of injustice, you produce . . . clever.

TOM: You know what is really thick-witted . . . getting caught in the tentacles of embezzlement. *(Laughs at his own joke)*

ERNEST *(to* LILLY*)*: See? Did you hear that, Lilly? He's doing it again.

LILLY: Come on, you two. This isn't helping anything.

ERNEST *(to* TOM*)*: You're having a giddy fit watching me squirm, aren't you?

TOM: You aren't an easy man to work with, Ernest. *(Pause)* Remember, be in Hastings' office in 20 minutes.

(TOM *exits through basement door.)*

ERNEST: I'm dead. No, I'm worse than dead. At least dead people don't have to stand in the unemployment line.

LILLY: You were pretty rough on Tom.

ERNEST: That annoying little rodent? He's not even worth my verbal squashing.

LILLY: Then what *is* worth something to you? Oh, I forgot . . . money.

ERNEST: Hey, I just had a flash. Maybe I could find a way to pin this whole thing on you.

LILLY: But you won't

ERNEST: And why not?

LILLY: Because I'll be praying that you won't.

ERNEST: Lilly and her faith. *(Pause)* So are you going to say it or what?

LILLY: Say what?

ERNEST: That my sins have found me out. Isn't that right on the tip of your tongue?

LILLY: Not quite.

ERNEST: Why not?

LILLY: Because I can see that you're already in pain.

ERNEST: Oh, it's nothing really . . . just a bit of life's irony trying to butcher my soul. *(Looking at his watch, and starting to get nervous)* And I have a bit of irony for you too. *(Pause)* Those documents you found were placed on top of your health food magazine . . . weren't they?

LILLY: How did you know that?

ERNEST: Because the Greek god of irony is up to his tricks again.

LILLY: Come on. Stop joking around.

ERNEST: I am my most serious when I'm joking.

LILLY: Are you going to tell me what's going on or not?

ERNEST: *I* am the one who put those documents in your desk!

LILLY: What?

ERNEST: I wanted you to find them . . . and I wanted you to turn me in. I couldn't do it myself, so I left the documents in your desk and then put copies in my assistant's file cabinet.

LILLY: I can't believe it.

ERNEST: Me either.

LILLY: If all this is true, then why have you been fighting the efforts to bring out the truth?

ERNEST: Because I thought of . . . the chance of prison. I don't think I can handle it. *(Pause)* Funny, I knew my assistant would turn me in before she took another breath, but you . . . you did surprise me.

LILLY: Because I came to *you* first?

ERNEST: Yeah. I guess that makes you a perfect white lily.

LILLY: I too have a secret I want to share with you.

ERNEST: Man, we've got more secrets than the CIA.

LILLY: Yeah, and we have more intelligence too.

ERNEST: That's very funny. I'd laugh, but I'm too busy planning my funeral. *(Pause)* So what is this secret of yours?

LILLY: Four years ago, while I was working at another ad agency, I experienced a sudden writer's block. It felt silly, but it was real. It just kept circling above my desk like a vulture, ready to devour my career.

ERNEST: Yeah, I guess I've had a couple of those. It was like I was sprayed down with idea repellent.

LILLY: Good analogy.

ERNEST: So what happened?

LILLY: One morning I saw a crumpled piece of paper by my wastebasket. It had notes scribbled all over it. On that discarded scrap of paper were all the perfect ideas for the campaign that I had been beating my brain over.

ERNEST: I take it you used those notes for more than a paper airplane.

LILLY: Yes. I used all the ideas on the note to launch a major campaign for a new toy company. Maybe you've heard of them . . . Weenie Woodles Fun Factory.

ERNEST: Yeah, I saw the commercials on TV. They were very original.

LILLY: But, none of it was mine.

ERNEST: It's shocking to imagine our perfect white Lilly with a broken petal. So did the owner of those notes step forward and sue you for plagiarism?

LILLY: No.

ERNEST: Well, then, you were home free.

LILLY: Not exactly. You see, I received an award and a raise because of my outstanding work on that project.

ERNEST: That's a problem? Excuse me, but I'm having a hard time drumming up any sympathy for you.

LILLY: The problem was that I knew in my heart it had not been my work at all. Someone else deserved that award and raise. Anyway, it ate at me, and over the next few weeks my work began to suffer, and I couldn't sleep at night.

ERNEST: Simple. You should have taken a sleeping pill.

LILLY: It's not that easy. I have a conscience.

ERNEST: I can take care of that too. Just take an anti-Christianity pill . . . then you can abort your guilt.

LILLY: That's quite a conversational epitaph for your tombstone someday, but it's one lousy, stinking way to live.

ERNEST: It hasn't been lousy . . . until now.

LILLY: Is that *you* talking . . . or your father?

ERNEST: I see you're going back to the meat grinder method again. *(Pause)* Who knows who's talking? I'm in a mental vacuum right now. I can't feel much except the throb from landing on my head instead of my feet.

LILLY: Why did you want us to turn you in?

ERNEST: I don't know why. Why did you tell me this little story about your fall from grace? *(Pause)* You never did explain what happened after you stole those campaign ideas.

LILLY: I told my boss what I'd done . . . and then I resigned.

ERNEST: You gave it all up that easily?

LILLY: It wasn't easy. Just as putting those documents in my desk wasn't easy for you.

ERNEST: I wish I hadn't now.

LILLY: I think some part of you is relieved.

ERNEST: Yeah, I'm relieved all right . . . relieved of my job and my life.

LILLY: You aren't going to die.

ERNEST: I'm already dead. They just haven't buried me yet.

LILLY: After this is all over, you will still have your education and your God-given talent. You can begin again. *I* did.

ERNEST: Spoken like a woman who obviously didn't do prison time.

LILLY: No, I didn't . . . but we're not certain you'll have to either.

ERNEST: I'd rather stay down here with these disease-ridden cockroaches for five years than spend five minutes in a prison. I'm used to entertaining clients . . . not axe murderers. *(Pause)* This is some crazy experience.

LILLY: What?

ERNEST: This journey into myself. I'm most definitely not having any fun. *(Looks at watch again)* Oh, joy, just 10 brief and eternal minutes, and I will be at their mercy. I'll probably have to give up my condo, my nightlife, and my little red sports car with the sunroof. I'll miss that most of all. I can really fly in that thing. My dad would have liked it. It has as much panache as he had. *(Pause)* But he wouldn't have liked this mess I'm in. In fact, he might have disowned me. He would have said, "My boy, you are an idiot. Idiots get caught, and you got caught. So, do you know what that makes you?" and I'd say, "Yes, Dad, that makes me an idiot."

LILLY: That doesn't mean you are.

ERNEST: We are all jesters pretending to be kings. *(Pause)* But my father . . . I think he must have been the king of kings when it came to pretending. *(Pause)* Once, when I was a kid, he pretended to be a celebrity on the bus, and some poor woman gave him 50 bucks for an autograph . . . just because she'd never met a famous person before. I asked my father why he did it, and he said, "I did it for a laugh." He always laughed a lot, but there wasn't any . . .

LILLY: Any what?

ERNEST: Nothing.

LILLY *(pause)*: You haven't said much about your mother.

ERNEST: I never knew my mother. She left right after I was born. I was raised solely by my father. *(Pause)* But now he's gone too.

LILLY: How did your father die?

ERNEST: No one really knows. Even the doctors were mystified. They finally mumbled something about a heart problem, but . . .

LILLY: But what?

ERNEST *(after a pause)*: I remember when my father was bedridden. Just hours before he died, he asked the housekeeper to go to the store and buy him another bottle of bourbon and a bottle of . . . peace. The housekeeper said he was just making another joke, but when she told him that the stores didn't have any peace to sell, my father got all red-faced and suddenly began to . . . to cry. He actually sobbed into his pillow like a little kid. I'd never seen him like that before. I didn't know what to do, so I just stood there next to him by the bed, as unbendable and empty as that bottle of bourbon on his night table. *(Pause)* Here was my father, dying . . . I mean really dying . . . and all I could feel was . . . embarrassment.

(Pause)

LILLY: That is a very sad story.

ERNEST: I never tell that stuff to anybody. There are reasons castles have drawbridges, I guess.

LILLY: I understand. I have one myself.

ERNEST: You know, I have this picture of Christians . . . cartoonlike cows grazing a field, bloating themselves on pretty-tasting church prattle. So why aren't you like that?

LILLY: Well, my doctor said I had to cut out grazing.

ERNEST: I like you, except I know you are trying to suck me into this hocus-pocus Christianity thing. I'm just not into unnecessary guilt.

LILLY: Christ isn't into condemnation.

ERNEST: So what's He into?

LILLY: Forgiveness and peace. Anybody can have it, no matter who they are or what they've done. All you have to do is acknowledge your sin, ask Him to forgive you and to come live in your heart.

ERNEST: Peace, huh. You know, I have to admit, you may be wound up like everybody else, but you sure don't tick the same. *(Pause)* I think maybe you're really trying to help me, and maybe some part of me is feeling not so good about what I've done, but I'm not quite ready for this. I have to think about it . . . real hard.

LILLY: OK.

ERNEST *(looks at his watch and rises to leave):* Well, I've got to go. The guillotine awaits. Wish me luck.

LILLY: I don't believe in luck.

ERNEST: So what are you going to do? Stay down here and work on that new dog deodorant commercial?

LILLY: No.

ERNEST: Well, what *are* you going to do?

LILLY: Pray.

ERNEST: For what?

LILLY: For you.

ERNEST: Well, I guess I can't stop you.

LILLY: No.

ERNEST: Maybe I don't really want to . . . stop you. Well, I have to go. *(He starts to go, then turns back to speak.)* I hope what you've said about God is for real.

LILLY: It is.

ERNEST: Because I have this feeling bourbon isn't going to get me through this. *(Opens the door to leave)* Good-bye.

LILLY: For now.

(ERNEST *smiles briefly and then exits stage left through basement door.* LILLY *bows her head to pray as the lights dim slowly to a blackout.)*

(Curtain)

Pokeweed and Mrs. Gasp

Cast of Characters

MRS. GLORIA GASP: A middle-aged widow who has a long-standing membership in her small community church. She is a Christian but has become lonely and bitter because of her husband's sudden death three years prior. There is a profound sincerity in Pokeweed's testimony that draws Mrs. Gasp back to repentance and peace.

POKEWEED JONES: A middle-aged single man who was nicknamed Pokeweed by his mother when he was a very young boy. Pokeweed has felt worthless all of his life, not because of his poverty, but because of his nickname. Through his conversion he is now able to recognize the preciousness of all people, including himself.

Scene

We are inside the sanctuary of a small community church. A pew sits center stage. The time is Sunday evening in the present.

Props

General:	Church pew
MRS. GASP:	Wristwatch
	Purse
	A pair of ladies' white gloves
POKEWEED:	Bible

At Rise

Mrs. Gasp is sitting in the middle of the pew, dressed and groomed immaculately. She wears a pair of ladies' white gloves.

(POKEWEED *enters stage left and sits down on the pew.* POKEWEED *is dressed in old tattered clothes and is carrying a Bible.* MRS. GASP *very subtly moves down the pew a few inches away from him.)*

POKEWEED: Howdy.

MRS. GASP: Good evening.

POKEWEED: They must have called off church 'cause of that rain out there.

MRS. GASP: In all the 15 years I've been a member of this church, they have never called off a Sunday evening service . . . even in questionable weather.

POKEWEED: Well, with all that raining and flooding outside, we sure got plenty of questionable. I expect to see Noah floating by any minute now. Yeah, sure does remind me of the rain of '67.

(Pause)

MRS. GASP: What happened during the rain of '67?

POKEWEED: Why, the rain was so heavy, it looked like a river coming down from the heavens. I heard some say that the fish got confused and tried to swim upstream to the clouds.

MRS. GASP: That is the most ridiculous thing I have ever heard.

POKEWEED *(smiles):* Ain't it though?

MRS. GASP *(looks at her watch):* I'm sure the pastor and some of the other members will be here soon. They're just running late.

POKEWEED: If you say so. *(Pause)* I'm not a member here.

MRS. GASP: I know.

POKEWEED: In fact, I've never been here before.

MRS. GASP: I know.

POKEWEED: Truth is, I've never been to church before in my life. Seems kind of crazy that the first time I decide to go to church, they call it off.

MRS. GASP: They haven't called if off.

POKEWEED: If you say so.

MRS. GASP: What made you decide to come *tonight?*

POKEWEED: God told me to come.

MRS. GASP: Just like that . . . God told you?

POKEWEED: That's right.

MRS. GASP: I don't think God talks to people that way.

POKEWEED: Then how does He talk to them?

MRS. GASP: I think God communicates more in chords than in sonatas.

POKEWEED: Well, I don't know much about music, but I do know that God told me to come tonight. Why? I don't know, 'cause they're bound to have called it off.

MRS. GASP: I'm sure people will be trickling in soon.

POKEWEED: If you say so. *(Pause)* Maybe we should introduce ourselves.

MRS. GASP: All right.

POKEWEED: You go first.

MRS. GASP: I'm Mrs. Gloria Gasp. I would shake your hand, but as you can see, I have gloves on. Ladies, I know, don't wear gloves to church anymore, but I always do. They preserve the dignity of the gathering. You may be interested to note that is why the Queen of England always wears gloves.

POKEWEED: Well, gloves or no gloves, it's a fine thing to meet you. I'm Pokeweed.

MRS. GASP: That is your full name?

POKEWEED: Pokeweed Jones, but everybody just calls me Pokeweed.

MRS. GASP: What an unusual nickname.

POKEWEED: My mama gave it to me.

MRS. GASP: I can't believe a mother would nickname her own son after some kind of . . . weed.

POKEWEED: The pokeweed blooms white flowers . . . but its root is poison. So Mama named me Pokeweed.

MRS. GASP: How terrible . . . to grow up that way.

POKEWEED: Yeah, but I only got a sprinkling of terrible. Some people get it poured all over them. *(Pause)* Anyhow, I sure did live up to the name Mama gave me. I became as ornery as a Louisiana gator. Once, just for meanness, I hooked up Farmer Cooney's outhouse to my truck and dragged it all the way down main street. They put me in jail for one whole year.

MRS. GASP: A year in jail. That punishment seems a bit harsh.

POKEWEED: Well, I thought so, too, until I found out Farmer Cooney was still in the outhouse when I hooked it to my truck.

MRS. GASP: And are you still?

POKEWEED: Still what?

MRS. GASP: Mean.

POKEWEED: Oh, no ma'am. That was years ago when I was unruly. I got over all that nonsense.

MRS. GASP: How did you get over it?

POKEWEED: Well, I took up drinking.

MRS. GASP: And do you still . . . partake?

POKEWEED: Nope. God done washed that meanness and boozing right out of me.

MRS. GASP: You can't use God like a crutch.

POKEWEED: Why not?

MRS. GASP: Because crutches are bad.

POKEWEED: Well, I figure leaning on God is a heap better than needing what was killing me.

MRS. GASP: So, I guess you haven't been a Christian long, then?

POKEWEED *(slowly, thinking):* Let's see. I'd say about twenty-three and a half . . .

MRS. GASP: Days?

POKEWEED: No . . . hours.

MRS. GASP: You mean you've only been a Christian for one day?

POKEWEED: Yep. And it's been the best day of my life.

MRS. GASP: You picked a gloomy time to become a Christian.

POKEWEED: Well, the sky says rain, but my heart says sunshine.

(Pause)

MRS. GASP: Was your mother a Christian?

POKEWEED: No. She was a Lutheran. *(Chuckles at his own joke)* Yeah, that was a good one.

MRS. GASP: You mean it was a joke?

POKEWEED: Why, sure. Hasn't anybody ever pulled your leg before? (MRS. GASP *is silent and looks a bit offended.)* No, I guess not. *(Pause)* No. My mama wasn't nothing when it came to God. But, oh boy, was she ever superstitious.

MRS. GASP: Oh?

POKEWEED: She couldn't ever leave the house on Mondays and Thursdays.

MRS. GASP: Why?

POKEWEED: Because she got it into her head that if she went out of the house on a Monday or a Thursday, she might kill somebody.

MRS. GASP *(very concerned):* Oh.

POKEWEED: Sometimes I think she wasn't right in the head.

MRS. GASP: I'm surprised you came out normal. *(Concerned)* You *are* normal, aren't you?

POKEWEED: I guess so.

MRS. GASP: Don't you know for sure?

POKEWEED: I don't know much for sure . . . except that God loves me. *(Pause)* Are *you* normal?

MRS. GASP: Yes, of course. What a question.

POKEWEED: Well, it's the same question you asked me. How would I know you weren't raised by a pack of hyenas if I didn't ask?

MRS. GASP: Maybe we should change the subject.

POKEWEED: Why?

MRS. GASP: Because you have to be careful what you say in God's house.

POKEWEED: Does that mean you don't have to be as careful what you say after you walk out the door?

MRS. GASP: What a question. *(Pause)* You know, I was just wondering . . . if you've never been to church before, then who came to your house and witnessed to you?

POKEWEED: God did.

MRS. GASP: That's not usually the procedure.

POKEWEED: Really? *(Pause)* Well, I sure am dumbfounded with all the stuff I got to know about God.

MRS. GASP: What do you mean?

POKEWEED: Well, since I've been here I've learned that God talks in chords, He doesn't make house calls, but if He does, don't tell Him any jokes, and don't talk about hyenas.

MRS. GASP: I will not be made fun of.

POKEWEED: Well, I'm just trying to figure out who I'm learning more about this evening . . . God . . . or you.

MRS. GASP: What a thing to say.

POKEWEED: Yeah, I guess we both got a lot to say. It's the rain outside. It brings out the secrets in people.

MRS. GASP: I've never heard of such a thing.

POKEWEED: It's true. The only reason you're talking to me is 'cause of that rain out there.

MRS. GASP: The only reason I'm talking to you is because you're the only person here.

POKEWEED: Well, I do like honesty. *(Pause)* I know I'm not much to talk to. My thinking parts aren't educated, and the rest of me isn't much to look at, so I guess maybe I was hoping for too much to make friends here.

MRS. GASP *(starts to speak but pauses):* I'm sorry if I offended you. I'm sure you'll make a friend here.

POKEWEED: Well, we all need friends . . . even me. I'll bet that preacher of yours would make a good friend.

MRS. GASP: Have you met him?

POKEWEED: Yep, some time ago he brought me a cake his wife had baked. He was real nice, but I told him to go on home 'cause I wasn't wanting to meet God yet. Later, when I was cutting into that cake he gave me, I found a box buried right in the middle. I opened it up, and inside was this teeny tiny little Bible. My sides hurt so bad from laughing, I thought I was passing a kidney stone. That preacher of yours, he has quite a sense of humor.

MRS. GASP: Yes, he is most certainly . . . unique. *(Pause)* Just a minute. I thought you said no one witnessed to you.

POKEWEED: He didn't. I wouldn't let him say a word about it, but God sure used him to reach me, and that is as true as it can be. *(Pause)* Yeah, until yesterday, life for me has been a whole lot of nothing. It seems like I've been living in a cave with some hollow echo where my heart should have been. I tried by my own wits and strength to dig out of that pit. I scratched and clawed till my spirit was bloody raw, but no matter how hard I tried, my own feelings held me there.

MRS. GASP: I don't understand.

POKEWEED: Feelings can create, and feelings can destroy . . . and this one was trying to do me in.

MRS. GASP: What was your feeling?

POKEWEED: That I had no place here on this earth. That I didn't even have enough worth to be alive.

MRS. GASP: So what happened yesterday to change your mind?

POKEWEED: Well, I opened up that Bible that the preacher hid inside my cake, and out fell a bookmark. On the front was a painting of a church with a field of flowers all around it. That picture couldn't have been any prettier. But, when I looked closer, I saw that there was weeds scattered all through those wildflowers. And those weeds—my, my, those weeds—they was standing straight up tall and smiling at the sun just like they really belonged there, glorifying God. And I thought, well Lord, maybe You could use an old weed like me after all.

MRS. GASP: But you're not a weed.

POKEWEED: You're right. That was what God told me, and it was the most tender thought I've ever known. I began crying like a baby. You see, I had never even imagined that I was precious to anybody . . . let alone to God Almighty. I gave Him my life right then and there, and He gave me His forgiveness. At that very instant, I no longer felt the misery of that cave . . . and I knew I wasn't born to be no pokeweed.

MRS. GASP: So why do you still go by that name?

POKEWEED: Well, tomorrow morning, ten o'clock sharp, rain or no rain, I'm heading to the county courthouse to find out the name I was given when I was born.

MRS. GASP: You mean you don't even know?

POKEWEED: Nope. I never did know my first name. Seems a real shame too. But it's a greater shame that I held off meeting God until yesterday.

MRS. GASP: I'm glad for you . . . that things are working out. *(Rises)* I think you were right. No one else is coming. They've called it off. *(Looks out toward audience as if looking through a church window)* The rain has gotten worse. I guess I'll have to wait till it settles down before I go home.

POKEWEED: Church must mean an awful lot to you to come out on an evening like this.

MRS. GASP: This service in particular was important . . . but I'm afraid I can't divulge why.

POKEWEED: Oh . . . OK . . . it's one of those. Yeah, everybody has got to have some of those kind of secrets, I guess.

MRS. GASP *(pauses before speaking):* I'm surprised you're not curious what the secret is.

POKEWEED: I am, but I figure that too much curiosity can get you in trouble. It's kind of like when you eat too many beans and franks.

MRS. GASP: What a thing to say.

POKEWEED: Oh. I reckon that's another one of those things you're not supposed to talk about in church.

MRS. GASP: No . . . I think not.

POKEWEED: Well, at least we're getting it narrowed down. Is there anything else I should know?

MRS. GASP: You should never make false accusations.

POKEWEED: Was I doing that?

MRS. GASP: No. But there are some people who do . . . in fact, there is one such person in this very church.

POKEWEED: Well, maybe the preacher should talk to that person about it.

MRS. GASP: The pastor can't do that.

POKEWEED: Why not?

MRS. GASP: Because he is the guilty party.

POKEWEED: That God-loving man? I won't believe that.

MRS. GASP: Are you implying that I am a liar?

POKEWEED: No ma'am.

MRS. GASP: Good.

POKEWEED: But I still don't believe you.

MRS. GASP *(sitting back down on pew):* I have proof. Exactly three weeks ago the pastor of this church came to my home and falsely accused me of . . . I can't even talk about it. It's too painful. All I can say is that a person should always hold onto their pride. God never expects us to give up our dignity.

POKEWEED: Well, dying on a cross sure wasn't dignified.

MRS. GASP *(wringing her hands):* Are you saying my life isn't biblically based?

POKEWEED: Well, I don't know much about the Bible . . . in fact last night was the first time I'd ever opened it, but what I remember reading was something about us being servants. And servants tend to get trampled and put through a lot of mess. Even Jesus had to put up with a lot of mess.

MRS. GASP: You simply don't have all the facts.

POKEWEED: If you say so.

(Pause)

MRS. GASP: I guess it's all right if I tell you. *(Pause)* Our minister actually had the gall to say that I was going around town spreading . . . I can't even say the word.

POKEWEED: Well, what were you spreading . . . manure or gossip?

MRS. GASP: I wasn't spreading anything.

POKEWEED: If you say so.

(Pause)

MRS. GASP: I want you to know here and now that I do not gossip. I merely transfer important information. *(Pause)* And please stop staring at me like that.

POKEWEED: I wasn't staring at you. I was looking out the window over there at the rain.

MRS. GASP: So is the rain getting worse?

POKEWEED: I don't know. The window is fogged over.

MRS. GASP: Then how could you be looking out the window if it's fogged over?

POKEWEED: I wasn't.

MRS. GASP: But that's what you said you were doing instead of staring at me.

POKEWEED *(flustered with* MRS. GASP): Well, I *tried* to look through that window over there, but when I looked over at *that* window over there, it was *fogged over.*

MRS. GASP: Oh.

POKEWEED: Why are you so all-fired worried about me staring at you. You got something to hide?

MRS. GASP: Of course not. It's just that to stare at someone is considered impolite.

POKEWEED: Well, I've been called a lot worse in my life, so that don't hurt me much.

(POKEWEED *scratches his head, thinking.)*

MRS. GASP: What are you scratching your head for?

POKEWEED: It ain't 'cause I got cooties, if that's what you're fretting about.

MRS. GASP: I'm not worried about anything.

POKEWEED: No? Then why are you wringing your hands? (MRS. GASP *remains silent.)* Tell you what . . . I'll tell you why I'm scratching my head if you'll tell me why you're wringing your hands.

Mrs. Gasp *(anger building):* I am not wringing my hands. *(Pause)* Maybe I am a little.

(Pause)

Pokeweed: Why would you come to church in this kind of weather when you don't even like the preacher?

Mrs. Gasp: Well, why did *you* come out? *(Slightly sarcastic)* Oh, I forgot, God told you to come.

Pokeweed: And He didn't tell you to come?

Mrs. Gasp: No . . . I mean, yes. I don't know what I mean. You're not a trial lawyer, you know. You're just a . . .

Pokeweed: A pokeweed?

Mrs. Gasp: You're just confusing me.

Pokeweed: I'm sorry.

(Heavy silence between them)

Pokeweed *(rises to go):* I guess I'd better go. Church is called off, and I guess I've caused enough trouble.

Mrs. Gasp: What about the rain?

Pokeweed: Oh, my old jalopy can plow through anything.

Mrs. Gasp: Oh.

Pokeweed: Can I give you a lift home? My old hearse is kind of dirty, but it'll get you there in one piece.

Mrs. Gasp: Did you say you drive a hearse?

Pokeweed: It was the only used car I could afford. The color is kind of depressing, but it's got great leg room. *(Pause)* Are you sure you don't need a lift home?

Mrs. Gasp: Thank you anyway, but I'm sure I don't ever want to ride in a hearse.

Pokeweed: Well, we all got to ride in one someday. *(Chuckles)* Well . . . good evening. *(He turns to leave.)*

Mrs. Gasp: Wait.

Pokeweed: What is it?

Mrs. Gasp: Could you sit down . . . please? (Pokeweed *sits down.)* I came tonight . . . because there was going to be a meeting of the deacons after the service. I am one of those deacons. And I was going to recommend that the pastor resign because of his questionable behavior.

POKEWEED: What did he do that was so awful?

MRS. GASP: I just explained it to you . . . his false accusations.

POKEWEED: That's it?

MRS. GASP: Yes, but . . .

POKEWEED: But what?

MRS. GASP: Oh my. Listen to that wind outside. I hate that lonely sound . . . don't you?

POKEWEED: I don't hear anything.

MRS. GASP: That sound reminds me of the day my husband died. It was three years ago . . . yesterday.

POKEWEED: Must have been a lot of wind and rain that day.

MRS. GASP: Oh, yes. There was a terrible storm. *(Pause)* And right during the worst of it, Walter, that was my husband, he looked out the window and saw a funnel cloud touching down. We both tried frantically to open some windows. That was what we had always been told to do . . . open windows. But they'd all been painted shut. I don't know if it was from the strain of pulling on those windows, or the fear of the tornado, but Walter, he all of a sudden fell to the floor. He was clutching his arm, and I knew he was having a heart attack. I wanted to get him into the car, but the tornado was coming right toward us. So, we just lay there in the hallway with our eyes closed praying. I just held him in my arms . . . waiting. When I opened my eyes . . . he didn't. He never did again. He'd died. And that tornado . . . that senseless act of nature didn't hit our house after all. I could see it through the patio doors pulling back up into the clouds and disappearing. People claim it was a miracle, but I didn't see any miracle for my Walter.

POKEWEED: But God saw fit to spare you.

MRS. GASP: But I miss Walter. Everybody does. He had so many friends. People just took to him naturally.

POKEWEED: Weren't they your friends too?

MRS. GASP: I thought they were. But after Walter died, I noticed that one by one all those same friends began falling away. At first they were supportive and kind. They baked things for me and would call to see if I was all right. But then gradually they didn't come around anymore, and they stopped inviting me to their homes. I realized then that they had all been Walter's friends . . . not mine.

POKEWEED: Don't you have any friends now?

MRS. GASP: Yes, I do. But they don't go to church here. I made new friends.

POKEWEED: That must have been hard . . . to start over making friends.

MRS. GASP: No. Actually it was easy, once I discovered what it was they wanted me to say.

POKEWEED: What was that?

MRS. GASP: Oh, little things . . . that say nothing . . . and yet everything.

POKEWEED: You mean . . . gossip.

MRS. GASP: You see, I couldn't seem to make friends like Walter could. He was always so good with people. He could make them laugh and feel good about themselves, but that didn't seem to work for me. One day when I was in town at the coffee shop, I happened to mention some tidbit about someone I knew. I guess they must have thought it was awfully interesting. Suddenly they thought *I* was interesting. One thing led to another. *(Pause)* Even though I know what it is they like me for, I can't seem to let go of my new friends. I'm afraid.

POKEWEED: What were you afraid of?

MRS. GASP: Of being all alone again.

POKEWEED: That's a sad thing. I sure am sorry.

MRS. GASP: I'm sorry too . . . only *I'm* sorry I told you all of this.

POKEWEED: Why?

MRS. GASP: Won't you just blab it to somebody else?

POKEWEED: Well, I have an allergy to blabbing . . . makes me break out in green hives.

MRS. GASP: That is the silliest thing I've ever heard.

POKEWEED: Ain't it though?

MRS. GASP: I am glad you're not going to tell anybody.

POKEWEED: Me too.

(Pause)

MRS. GASP: I suppose you think *I'm* the weed here.

POKEWEED: No. You're no weed either. Nobody is a weed. Maybe you're just a flower that's wilted a bit.

MRS. GASP: I guess that's a compliment.

POKEWEED *(friendly):* Yes, it was. You can thank me if you'd like.

MRS. GASP: Thank you.

POKEWEED: You're welcome. *(Pause)* You know, all wilted flowers need is a bit of water and sunshine to make them grow. What you need is a friend . . . a real friend.

MRS. GASP: That sounds nice, except I think *my* allergy is in making friends.

POKEWEED: I don't think so.

MRS. GASP: Why do you say that?

POKEWEED: Because I wouldn't mind being your friend. (MRS. GASP *is silent.)* Well, you know, I know it might be a little embarrassing to be seen being friends with me, so maybe we could just say hello when we see each other at church.

MRS. GASP: No, you wouldn't embarrass me. Well, maybe a little.

POKEWEED: I do indeed like your honesty, Mrs. Gasp.

MRS. GASP: You do?

POKEWEED: Yes, I do.

MRS. GASP: It is nice to have someone like something about me . . . something that is really me. *(Pause)* I wouldn't mind saying hello to you in church . . . and I wouldn't mind sitting with you from time to time . . . and I wouldn't mind too much . . . being your friend.

POKEWEED: If you say so.

MRS. GASP: I do say so.

POKEWEED: Well, I guess God didn't have me come tonight for nothing.

MRS. GASP: Maybe He had you come for more reasons than you know.

POKEWEED: What do you mean?

MRS. GASP: God did spare my life from that tornado. That's what you said, and that was true. I haven't wanted to face that fact . . . because, well, I just haven't. And because I haven't faced it, I've never thanked Him for that miracle. I was just thinking that maybe condemning the pastor for doing his job isn't the best way to show God my gratitude.

POKEWEED: That took a lot of courage to say all that.

(POKEWEED *rises and looks out the window.)*

MRS. GASP: You're leaving already?

POKEWEED: Well, I don't want to wear out my welcome.

MRS. GASP: Oh, but you can't wear out your welcome in church.

POKEWEED: No? That's good. I like that. That makes church like . . . heaven.

MRS. GASP: I guess church won't be heaven as long as there are people like me in it.

POKEWEED: Oh, now don't go saying things like that about yourself.

MRS. GASP: Now *you* be honest. When you first got here . . . that's what you thought about me, wasn't it . . . that I was a silly meddling woman?

POKEWEED *(thinks for a moment):* But now that I'm getting to know you more, I think you're all right.

MRS. GASP *(rises):* I guess that's better than people thinking I'm terrific for all the wrong reasons. Isn't that so, Mr. Jones?

POKEWEED: How come you didn't call me Pokeweed?

MRS. GASP *(smiles, looks out window as she removes her gloves):* The rain . . . it's stopped . . . finally.

POKEWEED: Well, the rain had to stop soon, 'cause the angels have tuned up their instruments and have started to sing.

MRS. GASP: How do you know the angels are singing? You're pulling my leg again, aren't you?

POKEWEED: Nope. I never joke about angels.

MRS. GASP: How do you know they're singing if you can't hear them?

POKEWEED: Well, God is good. I found the Lord, and we're going to be friends. Why wouldn't the angels be singing?

MRS. GASP *(looks out window again and agrees with a smile):* Yes . . . why wouldn't they?

(Curtain)

Love and Other Mysteries

Cast of Characters

JULIE APPLEBY: A happy, confident, high school teacher in her mid-20s. She teaches a myriad of subjects, but literature is her favorite. Julie's parents died two years apart when she was young. The grief was eased considerably because of her aunt and uncle's devotion and love for her. She cares for Harrison, but because she isn't certain they have a love that can last a lifetime, she hesitates marrying him. Julie speaks with a very mild Southern accent.

HARRISON: An easygoing high school teacher in his mid-20s. He teaches a variety of subjects, all of which he enjoys. What his personality lacks in romance, he makes up for with his keen sense of humor and understanding for what is worthwhile in life. He has doubts about marrying Julie, but his easygoing nature hinders him from seeing that there is something missing between them. He speaks with a very mild Southern accent.

MARTY: A fun-loving entrepreneur who made his fortune with a national chain of restaurants called "Marty's Gourmet Fish Cafés." He is impulsive, generous, and witty. He's an extrovert at heart with pockets of insecurity and shyness as well. He believes he loves Julie, but because it's been so long since he's seen her, he's not absolutely certain of his romantic feelings for her. Marty speaks with a very mild Southern accent, and occasionally uses a strong Irish accent for effect.

AUNT FAY: A kind-hearted woman in her 50s. Her folksy wisdom and childlike spirit give her personality a unique effervescence. She speaks with a mild Southern accent.

UNCLE BERNIE: A sprightly gentleman in his 60s. He is loving and romantic with just the right amount of mischievousness to make him intriguing. He speaks with a mild Southern accent.

Scene

Action takes place in a small Southern town on the front porch of the Appleby's house. The porch is old-fashioned and inviting. There's a long porch glider center stage and a rocking chair down right center. Other pieces of outdoor furniture may be substituted for the glider and/or rocking chair. The front of the porch faces the audience. There is a railing across the front porch with an opening down center, which leads to a footpath. Down right is a trellis covered with flowers, and stage left is a screen door leading to the kitchen offstage. A footpath runs parallel with the front of the porch, which leads to the driveway offstage. The play begins on an early summer morning in the present.

Props

General:	Outdoor furniture for porch
JULIE:	Large note pad
	Pencil
AUNT FAY:	Bowl of green beans
	Apron
	Materials to make lei: plastic flowers, needle, and string
HARRISON:	Small newspaper
	Large bowl of sauerkraut
	Large serving spoon
MARTY:	Small bouquet of violets

SCENE ONE

At Rise

Julie is seated on the porch glider, writing on a note pad. At first, Julie seems pleased with what she's written, but then frowns and scratches it out. She continues these actions while talking to Aunt Fay, who is in the kitchen, offstage.

JULIE *(loudly):* Aunt Fay? Are you still out in the kitchen?

AUNT FAY *(loudly from offstage left):* Yeah, I thought I'd snap a few beans.

JULIE: Need some help?

AUNT FAY *(sincerely):* No thanks. I enjoy it. Bean-snapping is sort of like a laxative for the mind. Helps me clear my thoughts. How's your poem coming along?

JULIE: I just decided something.

AUNT FAY: What's that?

JULIE: I decided that writing poetry is a lot like kissing a man.

AUNT FAY: What do you mean?

JULIE: Well, they both seem to come out better in my imagination.

AUNT FAY: Maybe you haven't kissed the right man yet. When I kissed your Uncle Bernie for the first time, it put a blush in my cheeks *and* my imagination.

JULIE *(continues to write and mark out words on note pad):* I guess I haven't had a good blush since Marty O'Malley kissed me in the third grade.

AUNT FAY *(enters through screen door, stage left, with bowl of green beans):* So, tell Aunt Fay all about the great romance in the third grade. *(She sits down on rocking chair and continues to snap beans.)*

JULIE: Well, after Marty kissed me, he proposed to me. Then instead of an engagement ring, he gave me his three dead goldfish.

AUNT FAY: Dead goldfish!

JULIE: He tried to be so romantic. I can still remember the pink satin bows he tied on the heads on those bloated little fish. Good ol' Marty. Last I heard he lived in Dallas and owned a fish market.

AUNT FAY *(lightheartedly):* At least he'll have plenty of dead fish when he starts courting those Dallas ladies. *(They both chuckle.)* So, is that the end of your story about Marty?

JULIE: Yeah, because for the next nine years Marty just made sheep's eyes at me from a distance.

AUNT FAY: Maybe dead goldfish plus sheep's eyes equal true love.

JULIE: If that's the case, then men plus love equals true mystery.

AUNT FAY: Yes, men can be a mystery. For instance, I have never understood why it is that men by themselves can be such gentlemen, but the minute you round 'em up into a herd, they all start squatting and spitting, and a thousand years of civilized behavior goes right out the window. *(They chuckle again.)* Come on, now. I want to hear your poem.

JULIE: OK, but you be honest. *(Rises from glider, goes to porch railing down left center)*

We met by chance
On that early summer morn.
His eyes reflected city lights,
While mine were country born.
He boasted of a fancy life.
While I said I loved country life.
He laughed and smiled,
And so did I . . .
Now he's a farmer boy,
And I'm his country wife.

AUNT FAY: Honey child, that is the sweetest poem that has ever graced these ears.

JULIE: Thanks. I assigned my students to write some poetry this summer, so I promised I'd write some too.

AUNT FAY *(rises from rocking chair and leans against railing down right center):* When that school hired you and Harrison, they got two living gold mines.

JULIE *(thoughtfully):* If it seems like I'm a gold mine, it's only because God has gilded my students with so much talent.

AUNT FAY: What a blessing you are, child. *(They smile at each other.)* Just take a whiff of that morning air. That's Trudy Mosel's roses sweetening up the breeze. *(She takes a deep breath.)* Mmmmm-mmm. That's enough to send me up to glory without even dying. *(Stretches to look down the street, down right)* Will you look at that. Trudy said she was tired of mowing her yard. Now she's got a cute little goat out there trimming her grass.

JULIE *(stretches to look down street, down right):* Looks like that goat's trimming her roses too.

AUNT FAY *(looks down street again):* Oh, no! He's eating up her prize roses. I'd better go tell her. Woo-oop. There she blows. Just like a cannon out the front door.

JULIE: She's going after him with a fly swatter.

AUNT FAY *(smiling):* Ooow yeah, and she's as mad as a freshly kicked bulldog. That goat is stew meat now.

JULIE: It looks like she's feeding something to him out of a jar.

AUNT FAY *(suddenly upset):* I'll tell you what she's feeding that worthless animal. That's my homemade pickled sauerkraut with chili peppers.

JULIE: How can you tell?

AUNT FAY: Honey, there are some things in this life you just know. *(Comically flustered)* But what I *don't* know is why she would give my finest pickled sauerkraut to a senseless beast that wouldn't know the difference between pig slop and pecan pie?

JULIE: Well, people have been finding a lot of creative uses for your sauerkraut.

AUNT FAY: Yeah, that's what everybody keeps telling me.

JULIE *(looks up the street, down left):* Look, there's Uncle Bernie. What's he doing with Mr. Potter up at the funeral home?

AUNT FAY: Oh, he promised to help Potter put some cow manure on his lawn to green it up. You know Mr. Potter. He loves to have people notice his funeral home as they're driving by.

JULIE *(pretends to hold her nose from odor):* Well, with a truckload of manure on his lawn, he's bound to get noticed.

AUNT FAY: Potter is quite a character. He loves talk like some people love drink. Of course, he really kicks into high gear if you mention anybody that's dead, dying, or even thinking about it. Sometimes he gets going and forgets to breathe. Once, I saw him turn blue from lack of oxygen. (JULIE *and* AUNT FAY *chuckle.)* Is Harrison coming over to see you this morning?

(HARRISON *enters on the footpath down right. When* HARRISON *hears his name, he stops and hides behind the trellis, smiling.)*

JULIE: I think so. He said he had something earth-shattering to talk to me about. *(Pleased)* He's going to ask me to marry him again, but I still haven't made up my mind.

AUNT FAY: You two have dated for nearly three years, haven't you?

JULIE: Yes. I'll get over my cold feet one of these days.

HARRISON *(comes out from behind the trellis):* Maybe I should buy you a warm pair of socks.

AUNT FAY: Oh, dear.

JULIE: Harrison. I didn't hear you drive up.

HARRISON *(lightly sarcastic to* JULIE): You see, it seemed like such a sunny and promising morning, I decided to walk. *(Friendly)* Hello, Mrs. Appleby.

AUNT FAY: Hello, Harrison. *(Pause)* Well, I'm feeling this powerful need to be somewhere else. I guess I'll just leave you two alone to thrash this out.

JULIE: See you later.

(AUNT FAY *exits through screen door.* HARRISON *steps onto porch with* JULIE.)

HARRISON: Maybe that's our problem. We don't thrash things out enough. I've always heard couples that love each other the most, argue the loudest.

JULIE: Well, I have to admit, Aunt Fay and Uncle Bernie can sure carry on sometimes . . . and I don't think there's another couple alive who love each other more.

HARRISON: You know, if you don't marry me this summer, I may have to take drastic measures.

JULIE: Like what?

HARRISON: Like . . . asking you again next summer. Who knows? Maybe I'll get lucky. Speaking of lucky, I'll tell you who has the luck of the Irish, and the blarney to go with it.

JULIE: Who's that?

HARRISON: Do you remember Marty O'Malley?

JULIE *(surprised):* Well, yeah. As a matter of fact, I was just talking about him this morning.

HARRISON: Really? Well, years ago he opened a fish business. Now he has a national restaurant chain called "Marty's Gourmet Fish Cafés."

JULIE: Those are all O'Malley's? I can hardly believe it.

HARRISON: Me neither. How can a kid grow up to own a famous chain of fish cafés when his entire youth was spent making spitballs out of glue. Makes you wonder what he's putting in the fish batter. (JULIE *gives* HARRISON *a wry look.)* I know that look of yours *(half-jokingly),* and no, I'm not envious of Marty's material wealth . . . his money, yes, but not his material wealth.

JULIE: Weren't you two best friends in school?

HARRISON: That's right. We fought like badgers, but we watched out for each other.

(UNCLE BERNIE *enters slowly up the footpath from down left. He is a sprightly gentleman in his 60s.* UNCLE BERNIE *is bent over with an aching back. He is wearing dirty overalls and is whistling happily.)*

JULIE: Uncle Bernie!

HARRISON *(with concern):* Mr. Appleby, do you need a hand?

UNCLE BERNIE *(looks at his hand and says jokingly):* Nope. My hand works fine. *(He chuckles.)*

JULIE: What happened?

UNCLE BERNIE: Well, I was playing this little game with the cow manure. I was trying to shovel it faster than Potter could talk. I lost. (AUNT FAY *enters through screen door. She allows screen door to slam shut to show her good-natured disapproval of* UNCLE BERNIE*'s activities.* UNCLE BERNIE *notices* AUNT FAY.) Uh-oh.

AUNT FAY: Ooo-weee! I didn't even hear you, old man. I just smelled you coming.

UNCLE BERNIE *(adoringly):* Ain't she sweet?

AUNT FAY: I hope you didn't sling the stuff at each other this time.

UNCLE BERNIE *(mischievously):* Well, it's just so tempting when it's farm fresh.

AUNT FAY: Get into the house, Bubba, and I'll fix your back. Then you can have some of my pickled sauerkraut.

UNCLE BERNIE: A bowl of that stuff ought to do me some good . . . (AUNT FAY *exits through screen door)* . . . if it doesn't kill me first. *(Chuckles)*

AUNT FAY *(hollers from offstage):* I heard that, you old buzzard!

UNCLE BERNIE *(to* JULIE *and* HARRISON): Ain't she sweet? *(To* AUNT FAY *offstage)* Coming, rosebud. *(To* JULIE *and* HARRISON *while exiting through screen door)* We've got a date tonight. We're going out stargazing.

HARRISON: Your uncle reminds me a little of Marty. I just wonder if he's up to something.

JULIE: Who?

HARRISON: Marty. I've barely heard from him since high school, and now he suddenly wants to come for a visit. Says he has something important to take care of here.

JULIE: So Marty O'Malley is coming for a visit. When?

HARRISON: Oh, yeah, we decided to meet over here at your house this afternoon.

JULIE: Oh really? Were you going to give me any warning, or were you two just going to show up on my doorstep like peddlers.

HARRISON: Well, I told you just now. Wait a minute. Are you mad at me? That's a good sign. Nothing like a good argument to put some hair on a relationship.

JULIE: We're not arguing.

HARRISON: Oh yes we are.

JULIE: No we're not.

HARRISON *(smiling):* See? I hear wedding bells already.

(JULIE *rolls here eyes upward and smiles.)*

(Blackout)

SCENE TWO

(Lights up on the Appleby's front porch. It is afternoon, the same day. HARRISON *is pacing thoughtfully up and down the footpath in front of the porch.* MARTY *suddenly rushes up the walk to greet* HARRISON. MARTY *wears bright clothes and a wild tie.)*

MARTY *(enthusiastically):* You old warthog. How you doing? Hey, remember the loyalty pledge we made in pig latin? (HARRISON *and* MARTY *both think for a second then yell out.)* Riendsfa orfa ifela! (HARRISON *and* MARTY *box at each other lightly in rhythm to the words and then end with a comical mannish bear clutch.)* Look at you. Except for that paunch and bald spot, you look just the same.

HARRISON *(jokingly):* And does everybody still call you Spittoon O'Malley?

MARTY: Only to my face. I'll bet I can still outspit you by a mile. Want to give it a try?

HARRISON: Naw, I'll take your word for it.

MARTY: So where's Julie?

HARRISON: I don't know. I knocked on the screen door, but nobody seems to be around. She knew we were coming, so I'm sure she'll be right back.

MARTY: We'll just have a sit on this fine old porch and wait for her.

(MARTY *and* HARRISON *move to porch.* HARRISON *sits on glider, and* MARTY *leans on railing.)*

HARRISON *(friendly):* So, tell me, are you disgustingly rich?

MARTY: Hey, I've got so much money, my banker comes to me for loans.

HARRISON: What's it like to be so wealthy? Is it exciting?

MARTY: Well, it's more fun than passing a kidney stone. Enough about money. Hey, how's your teaching? Is it still great?

HARRISON: Teaching teenagers . . . I don't know. Some days you wonder how you ever escape the jaws of insanity. *(Sincerely)* But, yeah, it is still great.

MARTY: And what about dear, sweet Julie? What's happening in her life?

HARRISON: The truth is, she finally caught me.

MARTY: What do you mean, she caught you? Are you talking about love or Montezuma's revenge?

HARRISON *(jokingly):* Maybe that's what love is . . . an emotional infection.

MARTY *(concerned):* So, is Julie in love with you?

HARRISON: Let me put it this way . . . I'm not sure if her emotional infection is as serious as mine. But it will be. Then she'll marry me. *(Pause)* You said you had something important to do while you're here. What's up?

MARTY: Oh. Actually, it's about . . . well, I'll just say it straight out. I have an incurable form of . . .

HARRISON *(concerned):* Of what?

MARTY: They're not sure. They just know it's . . . malignant.

HARRISON: What part of you is malignant?

MARTY: I don't know, here and there.

HARRISON: Here and there?

MARTY: Actually, in essence, it has some relevance to the uh . . . the uh . . . corpus luteum.

HARRISON: You have malignant ovaries?

MARTY: Oh. *(Realizing he's been caught in a lie)* I guess you wouldn't believe I caught it while I was on vacation in Mexico.

HARRISON *(cynically):* Got ahold of some real bad water, did you?

MARTY: OK. I'm sorry I lied. The actual reason I came for a visit was to make good on my promise to marry Julie. So, when you told me you were in love with her, I realized the only humane thing to do was to lie to you.

HARRISON *(rises and goes to railing):* Excuse me, let me correct something here. First, humane is for dogs, which I am not. And lies are for dirty dogs, which you are.

MARTY: OK, I'll give you that . . . if you'll give me Julie.

HARRISON: You can't barter for Julie like a boatload of fish. Besides, she's not for sale.

MARTY: I'm sorry, old buddy, but I love Julie too.

HARRISON: Since when?

MARTY: Since the third grade.

HARRISON: You couldn't even wipe your own nose in the third grade, let alone love somebody.

MARTY: Don't be cruel to a man who's helplessly in love.

HARRISON: Cruel? How about telling me you're dying so you can con me out of my girlfriend.

MARTY: I am sorry, old buddy. I've always loved you like a brother, but I love Julie more.

HARRISON: Well, I've got squatter's rights to Julie.

MARTY: Squatter's rights? If Julie's not a boatload of fish, then she sure isn't some chunk of homestead land.

HARRISON: I see. So, what's your game plan in romancing Julie away from me, now that you're not dying of malignant ovaries?

MARTY: I'm not sure. I can read women like a book, but the book is usually a mystery novel. Got any foolproof ideas?

HARRISON: Yeah, I've got this foolproof idea of putting you on a plane back to Dallas. Hold it. I don't know why I'm working up a sweat here. Give me one good reason why Julie would even go out with you.

MARTY: My unbridled charm.

(JULIE *enters the porch through the screen door, letting it slam shut.)*

JULIE *(excited to see* MARTY): Marty Spittoon O'Malley, it's great to see you and all your unbridled charm.

MARTY: Oh, boy.

HARRISON: So how long have you been standing there listening?

JULIE *(to* HARRISON): Let me put it to you this way. I don't think my emotional infection is as serious as yours.

HARRISON: How can you eavesdrop like that?

JULIE *(to* HARRISON): It's easy. I've been taking lessons from you.

MARTY: So how upset are you?

JULIE: Not much. To be perfectly honest, I thought you both were quite . . . comical.

HARRISON: Comical? Well, that implies witty and clever.

MARTY *(to* HARRISON): It also means idiotic and monkeylike. *(Said with a Irish accent to* JULIE) So, lassie, does this mean I won't be getting a *warm* "glad to see you" hug?

JULIE: It is good to see you again. (JULIE *and* MARTY *give each other a warm hug.)*

HARRISON: All right. That's *warm* enough.

JULIE: I have one tiny little question, since you're both mature adults. Well, at least you're adults anyway. Marty, if you loved me so much, why did it take you so long to tell me?

MARTY: I did tell you . . . in the third grade. Remember, I said someday when I made my fortune in the world, I'd come back for you . . . and marry you.

JULIE: I guess I do recall some of it.

MARTY: Do you remember what I gave you?

JULIE: You mean the three dead goldfish?

HARRISON *(to* MARTY): Yes, it's safe to say, old buddy, you are just crawling with charm.

MARTY: Hey, I was a poor kid, and those were my favorite fish.

JULIE: I thought the gift was rather touching.

HARRISON *(aside):* Boy, knowing that is going to save me a lot of money on Valentine's Day.

JULIE *(kindly):* Marty, we've never even been out on a date. How could you possibly know that you love me?

MARTY *(romantically):* The same way I know there is air to breathe and buttercups in the spring and nightingales to serenade us in the . . .

HARRISON *(interrupting):* Hello. Remember me . . . Julie's boyfriend?

MARTY: Listen, you were doubting Julie's love for you earlier. Maybe this is just the opportunity you've needed to test the strength of your relationship.

HARRISON: Marty, only you could make stealing somebody's girlfriend sound like a favor.

MARTY: What do you say, Julie? One date.

HARRISON: No cigar.

MARTY: I'm not asking for a smoke. I'm asking for a date. What do you say, Julie? If you don't fall in love with me after this one date, I promise never to bother you again.

(JULIE *considers the offer.)*

HARRISON: Julie . . .

JULIE: I'm sorry, Marty.

(MARTY *lowers his head sadly.)*

JULIE *(reacting to* MARTY*'s disappointment):* OK. Maybe.

HARRISON: Over my dead body.

MARTY *(pats* HARRISON *on the back and says humorously):* Hey, check with Potter up the street. Maybe he'll sell you one of those do-it-yourself burial kits.

HARRISON: Julie has a phobia for tasteless jokes. She'll never go out with you now.

JULIE: Well, I was thinking, maybe one friendship date would be all right.

HARRISON *(to* MARTY): Oh. All right, but friendship date means no mouth to mouth!

MARTY: But what if she chokes?

HARRISON: The only thing she'll be choking on is your blarney.

MARTY: Your blazing wit is about to singe my hair.

JULIE: I have another condition, please.

MARTY: Anything.

JULIE: Our date will be right here at the house, and Harrison is invited too. I'll make supper for both of you.

HARRISON: Why didn't I think of that?

MARTY: If Harrison comes along on the date, then I won't have a level playing field.

HARRISON: Well, you have the advantage of being rich, so that ought to even out our handicaps.

JULIE: Is this going to be a date or a golf match?

MARTY *(said while bowing to* JULIE*)*: It will be a date, and one we shall never forget.

HARRISON *(impishly):* I couldn't have said it better.

(Blackout)

SCENE THREE

(Lights up. It is evening, the next day. AUNT FAY *is standing by the porch railing with a long string of flowers. Three more flower heads remain on the railing, which will finish her lei. It is obvious to the audience when* AUNT FAY *first speaks that she has been playing "He loves me; he loves me not" each time she adds a flower head to the string.)*

AUNT FAY *(picks up a flower head, adds it to the string with her needle and says):* He loves me not. *(Adds another, and so on)* He loves me. He loves me not . . . *(Changing her mind about the ending)* . . . not as much as he'll love me when I give him this. *(Smiles, satisfied with her new ending and her lei)*

JULIE *(entering through screen door wearing an attractive dress):* What are you making? *(Leans against railing)*

AUNT FAY *(ties the string together, making a necklace of flowers):* It's a necklace out of sweet-smelling flowers to hang around your Uncle Bernie's neck. Tonight when he comes home from spreading manure, I'll be armed and ready.

JULIE: I guess you know I'm in love with the way you two are in love.

AUNT FAY: Me too. Loving your Uncle Bernie is like taking a trip on one of those big balloons . . . you don't mind being carried along with a little hot air, when you're having the ride of your life. I have the good Lord to thank for that ride, and I do every day.

JULIE: My parents had a love like yours and Uncle Bernie's, didn't they?

AUNT FAY: Yes, indeed, God rest their souls, your parents had so much love for each other, that just watching them together made your heart ache with joy.

JULIE: I want the same for my own marriage. Do you think I'm hoping for too much?

AUNT FAY: No, because marriage with the right man can be a kind of splendor, and marriage with the wrong man can become a kind of misery.

JULIE *(after a thoughtful pause):* Well, I guess Marty and Harrison will be here soon.

AUNT FAY: Honey child, I still can't get over all of that. Here just yesterday you were talking about you and Marty in the third grade, and now here he is again coming to see you. Sometimes life just seems like a picnic basket full of surprises.

JULIE: I just hope *this* picnic basket isn't sitting on an anthill.

AUNT FAY: Whatever happens, it is sure to be an evening to write about. And a pretty one too. Your Uncle Bernie told me to watch the sky tonight. He says the stars will be as flashy as the baubles on a dime-store floozy. Oh, I'd better get going. I have to make my deliveries tonight.

JULIE: How many more jars of sauerkraut did you sell?

AUNT FAY: I sold 30 more jars. Folks are saying now that it even cures baldness and bunions. And Riley Tuttle even claims it saved his marriage.

JULIE: Riley Tuttle? The town's auctioneer?

AUNT FAY: That's right. Anyway, Mr. Tuttle had a problem with auctioneering out loud in his sleep.

JULIE: That doesn't sound bad enough to break up a marriage.

AUNT FAY: Well, maybe not, but it was his wife he was trying to auction off.

JULIE *(chuckles):* So how did your sauerkraut help him?

AUNT FAY: He started eating it before bedtime, and now instead of auctioneering in his sleep, he just tosses and turns all night. *(They both chuckle.)* Now you tell Marty and Harrison I said howdy-do. I'm taking the jalopy out back. See you later. *(Takes lei and exits through screen door)*

JULIE: Bye-bye.

(After a pause, MARTY *enters on footpath, down right. Except for his tennis shoes, he is dressed formally in black tails, bow tie, etc., and is carrying small bouquet of violets.)*

MARTY: Hello. You look just like a peach. *(He joins* JULIE *on porch.)*

JULIE *(sweetly):* Are you insinuating I'm plump and fuzzy?

MARTY *(with Irish accent):* No, lassie, I'm meaning soft and sweet.

JULIE *(sincerely with Irish accent):* And you, laddie, look grand, like the groom dressing up the top of a wedding cake.

MARTY: These are for you.

JULIE *(accepting violets from* MARTY*):* Violets are for the month I was born.

MARTY *(romantically):* I know.

JULIE: Thanks.

MARTY: Look, I know this isn't right . . . me trying to romance you away from Harrison, but if it counts for anything at all, I've loved you a lot longer than he has.

JULIE *(gently):* Since the third grade?

MARTY: You don't believe me, do you?

JULIE: Why didn't you ask me out when we were in school?

MARTY: Fear.

JULIE *(kindly):* You were afraid? Of me?

MARTY: It took me all these years to get up the courage to come and see you. I guess I found courage in having lots of money. I confess I've been using opulence like putty . . . always trying to fill in my imperfections with it. But when you face someone you care about, then you have to face yourself. It's then you realize the putty is just a cheap fix. You and Harrison are different. You have a true courage. The kind that chooses a profession that benefits people instead of one's pocket.

JULIE: I'm afraid our great white courage has a big ugly stain on it . . . called envy. And since we're on a confessional roll here, there's something else I want to tell you. *(Pause)* I'm afraid I might hurt Harrison.

MARTY: How?

JULIE: What if I fall in love with you?

MARTY: That's pretty crazy. Maybe we should both be committed . . . to each other.

JULIE: But maybe we're not looking at the . . .

*(*JULIE *is interrupted by* HARRISON *whistling happily. He enters on the footpath, down right. He is dressed in dirty work clothes.)*

HARRISON *(to* MARTY*, lightheartedly):* You rascal, you got here before I did. And I know what you're up to with those flowers and that penguin suit.

*(*HARRISON *does the following while* JULIE *speaks. He wipes his foot on the ground as if to remove some manure. He looks at the bottom of his shoe, tries shaking his foot, and then gives up, shrugging his shoulders.)*

JULIE *(to* HARRISON, *while smiling and covering her nose):* Harrison! What in the world have you been doing? You smell like a . . . a . . .

MARTY: Like the slime in a sewer swamp.

HARRISON *(to* MARTY): Good alliteration. *(To* JULIE) Yes, I've been sharing with your uncle and Mr. Potter the fine art of spreading manure.

MARTY *(sarcastically):* I forgot you were such a Renaissance man.

HARRISON: Sorry, I didn't take a shower. *(Sly smile)* Oh, dear. I hope this doesn't *foul* up the evening. *(Sniffs the air)* Is that homemade dumplings I smell for supper? Mmmm-mmm. *(Heads toward the screen door)* Come on. Let's eat it up before it becomes bacteria and decides to eat us.

MARTY *(sarcastically):* Oh, goody. Now we can all eat with gusto.

(JULIE *chuckles at* HARRISON, *pats him on the back, waves her hand because of the smell, and then shakes her head, smiling.* HARRISON, JULIE, *and* MARTY *exit through screen door.)*

(Blackout)

SCENE FOUR

(Lights up. Two hours later on the same evening. MARTY, HARRISON, *and* JULIE *enter through screen door.* HARRISON *is carrying a small newspaper.)*

HARRISON *(rubs his stomach and sits on glider):* Now, that was a meal. *(Kiddingly)* Yeah, those dumplings stuck together like long lost friends. *(Changes reference to* MARTY'*s continual attempts to win* JULIE) But, in reality, it was just one giant dough ball with no concept of friendship, because *it* was really a traitor about to embark on a romantic encounter that would lead to nothing but folly and ruin.

MARTY *(lightly):* You experienced all of that in a plate of dumplings? Amazing. You should have somebody write that down . . . perhaps in a mental health facility.

HARRISON *(mouths* MARTY'*s words silently in mocking fashion behind him as* MARTY *goes to porch railing):* Perhaps in a mental health facility.

JULIE *(sits on glider with* HARRISON *and takes his hand):* What am I going to do with you two?

HARRISON: How about marrying me and throwing him to the sharks?

MARTY: Hey, no proposing to my date.

HARRISON: She may be your date, but she's my girlfriend.

JULIE *(lightly):* You know, at the rate you two are regressing, you may be going home in baby carriages.

MARTY: You're right. I apologize.

HARRISON: So do I.

MARTY: By the way, Julie, supper was truly an inspiration to the senses . . . except for the lingering odor of cow manure. Honestly, Harrison, you smell worse than rotten fish.

HARRISON: Well, you should know about rotten fish. You serve enough of it in your restaurants.

JULIE *(exasperated at* HARRISON *and* MARTY *for arguing):* Hey! I'm declaring a cease-fire right now, so you men put away your guns, or I'll . . . send you home without your cookies and milk. *(Gazes up at the sky)* We should be enjoying these stars. *(Rises from glider and goes to railing)* The sky is pure poetry tonight. (MARTY *gazes up at the stars with* JULIE.) You know, Shakespeare called the stars "the burning tapers of the sky."

MARTY: And Milton called them "living sapphires."

HARRISON *(comically defensive since he doesn't have a quote):* Yeah, well, I just call 'em stars.

JULIE:

When at last the night clouds opened
We did not begrudge the wait,
For divine delight was offered
In the fireworks at heaven's gate.

HARRISON: Now I like that one. Who wrote that?

JULIE: I did.

HARRISON: No wonder I liked it.

JULIE *(points to the sky):* Look, up there. It's a blimp!

(HARRISON *rises and watches blimp with* JULIE *and* MARTY.)

MARTY: It's headed this way.

JULIE: I wonder what a blimp is doing way out here.

HARRISON: Maybe it lost its mommy.

JULIE: Look. It has moving lights. Must be an advertisement. *(Reads sign slowly)* It says, "Life is a rose when you're in love's garden." *(To* MARTY) That's pretty . . . and pretty suspicious.

HARRISON *(to* MARTY): OK, we know you sent the blimp, but it won't work, because Julie is a modern woman . . . unimpressed with such pretentious frivolity. Go ahead, Julie, tell him off.

JULIE: Well, it was a bit impractical, but it was also poetic and imaginative and romantic.

HARRISON *(sarcastically):* That's telling him, Julie.

JULIE *(to* HARRISON): I'm not finished. *(To* MARTY) But under the circumstances, it might be considered . . .

MARTY: There's no need to continue, because I didn't even send the blimp.

HARRISON: Now let me get this straight. That flying hot dog up there just happened to be cruising over the neighborhood with a love note on it.

JULIE: Harrison, did you send it?

HARRISON: Me? Hire a blimp on a teacher's salary? That's like paying the national debt with parking meter change. *(Returns to glider and opens newspaper)*

MARTY *(to* JULIE): I may not have sent that message, but it did express my sentiments.

HARRISON: Objection.

MARTY *(moving closer to* JULIE): Objection overruled.

HARRISON *(turns down the corner of this newspaper and peers over the edge suspiciously):* Looks like it's time for a recess and two heaping bowls of Aunt Fay's famous pickled sauerkraut.

JULIE: Harrison, that's not a good idea.

MARTY: Your Aunt Fay makes pickled sauerkraut?

HARRISON: That's right. It's her very own recipe. And she'd be mighty offended if you didn't try some.

JULIE: Harrison.

MARTY: No, I'd like to try it. Really.

HARRISON: Let me take care of that right now.

JULIE *(squinting her eyes in displeasure at* HARRISON): None for me, thanks. I'm on a low sauerkraut diet. (HARRISON *exits through screen door.)* I'd better warn you, my aunt's sauerkraut has a unique quality to it. Sort of like spontaneous combustion.

(MARTY *takes* JULIE *by the hand and sits her down next to him on the glider.)*

MARTY: I just wanted to be alone with you for a minute.

JULIE: Oh.

MARTY: I know I'm way out of order, but . . . I would like to kiss you.

JULIE: But what about Harrison?

MARTY *(kiddingly):* I don't want to kiss Harrison.

JULIE: You know what I mean.

MARTY *(seriously):* So, are you going to marry him?

JULIE: I don't know.

MARTY *(with Irish accent):* Well now, darling, if you marry him without ever pressing your lips to mine, we'll always be tormented . . . wondering if that one kiss would have changed our lives forever.

JULIE: Harrison's right. You have a gift for making disloyalty look like a good deed.

MARTY: OK. I admit it. I'm despicable. I'm a pile of roach droppings. I'm a sardine hiding in the caviar. *I* am a double helping of castor oil.

JULIE: You forgot thick-necked troglodyte.

MARTY: And all my relatives are thick-necked troglodytes, too, but I still want to kiss you.

JULIE: And I want to kiss you.

MARTY: Well, here goes . . . destiny.

(MARTY *and* JULIE *pucker their lips and slowly move closer and closer until their lips meet in a comical kiss. They both separate, lean back in the glider with odd expressions, and then burst into laughter.)*

MARTY: So, was it the same for you.

JULIE: Like kissing my brother? Yes.

MARTY: Yeah, me too, and I don't even have a brother.

(JULIE *and* MARTY *laugh again.)*

HARRISON *(enters through the screen door with a large bowl of sauerkraut and a very large spoon):* Here we are. So, was the joke a good one?

JULIE: Oh, Marty and I were just examining the false concept of *destiny.*

HARRISON: That's nice. As long as you two weren't out here kissing.

MARTY: We did a little of that too.

HARRISON: What? You did what? I knew I couldn't leave you two alone for a minute. I should have reminded Julie that you've won every spitting contest since the day you were born. That would have put Julie in a really romantic mood, but no, I didn't because I trusted my old buddy from high school.

MARTY: If you trusted me, *old buddy,* you wouldn't have employed the five-alarm sauerkraut.

JULIE *(goes to* HARRISON *and holds his arm):* I am sorry it hurt you, but Marty and I did find out something important.

MARTY: We discovered we care about each other, but not in the wedding cake sort of way.

HARRISON: Oh. That's great. That means I'm still in the running.

JULIE *(gently):* But Harrison, it isn't a contest . . . it's a . . . well, it's . . .

HARRISON: Yes?

JULIE: It's like a color wheel.

HARRISON: A color wheel?

JULIE: I don't know. When we're together, we're like yellow and blue.

HARRISON: Yellow and blue make green. Green is a nice color. What are we talking about here? Love or art?

JULIE: Both. When you leave out one of the primary colors of the spectrum, the artist may never paint the masterpiece.

HARRISON *(disappointed):* So what are you saying? Our relationship is missing a primary color? *(Romantically)* How about if I buy us one of those jumbo boxes of crayons and I let you have all the red ones. If it's romance you want, I'm willing to do all that stuff. I can wear penguin suits and recite Shakespeare.

JULIE: It isn't that. You are romantic in your own special way. Actually, if you'll recall, you've had your doubts about us marrying too.

MARTY: That's true, but I really like being with you.

JULIE: You know, while we're waiting to solve the mysteries of love and marriage, maybe we could enjoy three perfectly good friendships.

HARRISON: I guess that idea isn't totally offensive.

MARTY *(goes to* JULIE *and* HARRISON *and throws an arm around each of them):* This is great. *(To* HARRISON) So what do you say, old buddy? Are we still "Riendsfa orfa ifela"?

HARRISON: Oh, all right, but only after you eat a big spoonful of Aunt Fay's sauerkraut.

JULIE: Harrison!

MARTY: No, he's right. It will settle the score. *(Takes the bowl of sauerkraut from* HARRISON *and prepares to take a bite)* So, here's to three incredible friendships and one incredible bowl of pickled sauerkraut.

(MARTY *eats a big bite of sauerkraut.* JULIE *and* HARRISON *wait for his reaction. At first* MARTY *seems as though he can't breathe.)*

JULIE *(concerned):* Marty, are you breathing? *(Takes the bowl and spoon from* MARTY)

MARTY *(swallows loudly and then pauses with a wide-eyed expression):* It's absolutely mouth-boggling. I've never experienced anything like it. All we'd have to do is put the word *gourmet* on this stuff, and with a little luck, someday your aunt and uncle could be rich.

JULIE: Well, my aunt always did say she wished she had enough money to buy Uncle Bernie a big telescope for stargazing. *(Looks up at sky)* Look! The blimp is headed back.

HARRISON: Look what it says now.

(HARRISON, MARTY, *and* JULIE *stand by railing to watch the blimp.)*

JULIE *(reads lighted sign on blimp with joy):* "To my rosebud, Fay . . . Love forever . . . From your old Bernie"

MARTY: Like I said, maybe someday *I'll* be as rich as your old aunt and uncle.

(Curtain)

The Beauty Operator

Cast of Characters

PEARL: A generous, intelligent, and humble character. She is fairly attractive, single, and 41 years old. She is the sole proprietor of the beauty shop, and its only employee. Even though she was born in Oklahoma, she has very little accent. Pearl is a little surprised, but very pleased that her friendship with Matthew has taken a romantic turn.

MISS ROSE: A 75-year-old with one sister and two brothers. She had one great love in her life, but he died before they were old enough to marry. She likes to wear flowery dresses in pastel shades with matching accessories. She enjoys embroidery and bird-watching. She is an intelligent woman, with a tendency to say exactly what's on her mind, yet she is beginning to show signs of forgetfulness.

CHARMANE: A 30-year-old, slightly overweight woman with a heavy Oklahoma accent. She chose not to attend college, because her parents could not help her financially and was unsure whether she could maintain her studies, since she didn't perform well in high school. Charmane is not simple-minded but is not able to articulate her deeper thoughts. She is happy and outgoing at times, while at other times withdrawn and insecure. She enjoys her marriage to Randall and hopes to have children soon.

REBECCA JONES: An ambitious, 24-year-old, single, career woman. She works as an account executive at an advertising agency in Dallas. She grew up on a farm three miles west of Noley. Attended one of the universities in Oklahoma City. She has very little accent because she has attempted to eliminate it from her speech. She comes from Dallas to visit her parents, but avoids the townspeople as much as possible because she is offended by their references to her as cute, little Becky Jones. She wants to attend the Hammond wedding for two conflicting reasons: to face her grief head-on and to continue the fantasy that she can somehow stop the wedding.

MATTHEW STEVENS: A 45-year-old wheat farmer. He's honest, kindhearted, and hardworking. He's a widower of five years with no children. Over the past few months Matthew has taken a romantic interest in Pearl.

Scene

Action takes place in 1973 at Pearl's Beauty Parlor in Noley, Okla., a small farming community. Pearl's is quaint and colorful. The beauty equipment and shop furniture are old-fashioned even for the early 1970s. Swivel beauty chair and mirror are downstage right center. Two dryer chairs and the rinsing chair are upstage center. An open doorway in the left wall upstage leads to a hallway and closet. Comfortable waiting chair and magazine table are stage left. The main shop entrance is downstage left. An imaginary picture window faces the audience.

Props

General:	Beauty shop equipment: swivel beauty chair; counter and large mirror for wall; one or two dryer chairs; rising chair with sink; waiting chair; magazine table or rack; ladies' magazines; closet (may use a folding partition); small footstool or step stool; etc. (If major beauty shop equipment cannot be acquired, other chairs may be substituted.)
PEARL:	Watch Plastic cape Two applicator bottles (for perm solutions) Electric rollers and clips Brushes Combs Wave rods and tissue paper (for perm) White towel to tuck in collar under cape Timer
CHARMANE:	Tabloid Purse
REBECCA:	Purse Watch
MISS ROSE:	Tea bag Purse Compact Handkerchief Hairnet Gaudy pillow with embroidery work Bag for pillow Embroidery needle and thread Timepiece for blouse (or watch)

Sound Effects

Train
Bell for shop door
Tumbling of boxes and general noise from closet

At Rise

Charmane's face is buried in a tabloid from the grocery store while she sits in the beauty chair. Pearl, the beautician, is rolling Charmane's hair in wave rods and papers for a permanent. Miss Rose, another patron, is seated on one of the dryer chairs and is fussing in her purse, looking for a handkerchief and compact.

CHARMANE *(turns pages of tabloid with great interest and then spots an intriguing headline):* Oh, hey, listen to this right here. "Aliens from outer space help young woman find herself." *(Pause)* Boy, is that strange! How could a woman lose herself?

(PEARL *rolls her eyes upward in amused exasperation.)*

MISS ROSE: The only thing those papers are good for is to line the bottom of my bird cage.

CHARMANE *(defensively):* Well, I think they're real educational. I've read these things for years and I haven't never been hurt by them. *(Embarrassed, she slips the tabloid under her purse.)* Pearl, if you make those wave rods any tighter, I'll have a permanent smile. Hey, I made a pun. You know, my husband always says that's when I'm my funniest, is when I don't try. But somehow I think he's making fun of me when he says that. I'm never sure. *(She laughs but is unable to hide all the hurt.)* Sometimes I cry because I can't figure it out.

PEARL *(encouragingly):* You know Randall loves you. I heard him say so at the church fair last week.

CHARMANE: That's right. He did, didn't he. He said it in front of everybody over the big mike. I thought it was real romantic of him. I remembered what he said too. I memorized it for prosperity.

MISS ROSE *(to* CHARMANE): You mean for posterity.

CHARMANE: Oh. Well, anyway, I memorized it. Randall said, "Wild plums sure are sour, but my Charmane's as sweet as a flower. My love for her doesn't fade, even though today we've been married one whole decade."

MISS ROSE: I remember him doing that. It came right after the cow chip throwing contest. *(Powders her nose and dabs her chest with her handkerchief)*

CHARMANE: Now I kind of wish Randall could have thought of some other word to rhyme with fade instead of decade. It makes me feel so *old.*

MISS ROSE *(stuffs her handkerchief in her sleeve and says lightly):* Watch your language. What's so awful about being old. *I'm* old.

PEARL *(after a silence from* CHARMANE *speaks up sincerely):* Well, you know the saying, "You're as young as you feel."

MISS ROSE: Well, I guess I don't feel all that young, come to think of it. I know why nobody wants to be old. Because you don't want to wake up one morning and realize you can't hide the wrinkles anymore. Or you can't remember where you put your false teeth or your heart medicine. Or you watch a youngster cheat you out of your two-dollar change at the dry goods store because he thinks you're too old and senile to notice. Or maybe your relatives think you'd be better off selling the only home you've known for the last 75 years to put you in some room that smells like disinfectant at the Green Meadows Nursing Home. You know they wash the place down with that stuff so you can't smell what's really going on there . . . people dying from nothing to do except finger-paint on little paper plates. Of course, then they take the silly tacky things and put them up all over your walls. That's to convince visitors you're having a gay old time down at the nursing home.

CHARMANE *(picks up the tissue papers on the counter and hands them to* PEARL *as she needs them for the permanent):* I've heard Green Meadows is a pretty nice place.

MISS ROSE: It's nice and pretty all right. Nice and pretty as a funeral parlor. Maybe you'd like to come visit me when my relations sell me down the river to that place.

PEARL *(turns to* MISS ROSE): Miss Rose, I've known your sister and brothers for a long time. They don't seem like the type to do that to you.

MISS ROSE: Maybe not, but a friend of mine, you know her too, Maggie Spencer. Well, anyway, she thought her family wasn't that way either, and there she is at Green Meadows. That woman was happy working her garden and loving life till they put her in that place. Last time I saw her they had her strapped to a chair with a bedsheet. She didn't even know who I was. I can tell you right now, there's nothing spookier than looking into your best friend's eyes and then realizing there's nobody there anymore.

PEARL: Mrs. Spencer used to come in here every week to get her hair fixed, never failed. She always told me she'd been blessed with a long, happy life.

MISS ROSE: That's true. She did have a happy life. I have to admit, she does seem really peaceful down there at that nursing home . . . but her husband seems peaceful too, and he's six feet under at the Noley graveyard.

PEARL: Sometimes life can be pretty unpleasant. But we all know Mrs. Spencer is a fine Christian woman, and we all know where she's headed someday. So, I suppose, in the *long* scheme of things, I don't pity her. And knowing her, I don't think she'd want me to.

MISS ROSE: Maybe you're right, Pearl. I've been looking at this from the wrong end. Maybe I'm in more torment over her condition than she is.

CHARMANE *(nonchalantly):* Yeah, torment can sure be a nasty thing. I've got neighbors who live in torment. They could have some peace, but now I think they've gotten too happy with torment to change.

MISS ROSE: Mercy me. You mean those Hendersons are still at it after 25 years of marriage?

CHARMANE: Why, they still argue over how much grind to put in the percolator.

MISS ROSE: Isn't that just the way things go.

CHARMANE: Our kitchen windows face each other. One time I actually saw a two-quart pan flying across the window at Mr. Henderson. The reason I know it was a two-quart pan and not a one-quart pan is that Mrs. Henderson loaned me her one-quart pan because mine was catching a drip in the living room after that big rainstorm we had last . . .

MISS ROSE *(loudly):* Well, did she hit him?

CHARMANE: I think she must have, 'cause I saw Mr. Henderson later with a big bandage over his forehead.

MISS ROSE: My stars and purple garters, someday that woman's going to kill him dead!

*(*REBECCA *enters through the main shop door, downstage left. A tiny bell rings as the door swings open. All the attention is suddenly on* REBECCA. *She is dressed in a stylish business suit.)*

REBECCA: I'm sorry, I don't have an appointment, but I was hoping you could help me. I'm supposed to be in a wedding in an hour or so, and I'm afraid I got caught in a cloudburst earlier. My hair is dry now, but it needs some hot rollers. Do you *have* electric rollers here?

MISS ROSE *(proudly):* She most certainly does. Pearl's Beauty Parlor was the first in this whole area to get those newfangled things. Nobody can say our little town's behind the times.

PEARL *(friendly):* It's no problem to roll your hair, but there might be a little wait. *(Sincerely)* I'm sorry.

REBECCA: I don't have a lot of time. Is there another salon here in town? *(Looks at her watch nervously)*

CHARMANE: Nope. Pearl's is the only beauty parlor in Noley. I guess you'll just have to wait.

MISS ROSE: I don't mind waiting. You can go ahead of my shampoo and set. I'd hate to think you'd miss being in a wedding just because I want to look beautiful. *(Readjusts her hairnet)*

REBECCA: Thank you.

MISS ROSE: You're more than welcome. It's like I always say . . . It's good for the soul to help an outsider.

(REBECCA *looks over magazines on table, takes one, and sits down on waiting chair.* REBECCA *looks up and sees* MISS ROSE *and* CHARMANE *staring at her.* MISS ROSE *and* CHARMANE *quickly look away.* REBECCA *flips through magazine briskly.)*

CHARMANE *(while looking* REBECCA *over again):* I guess you're here for that big Hammond wedding up at the Methodist Church.

REBECCA: That's right.

CHARMANE: Well, I was invited, but I'm not going. I had a falling out with the bride-to-be.

PEARL *(still working on* CHARMANE'*s hair):* Charmane, are you still upset with Lisa because your dresses were just alike at the prom? That was more than 10 years ago, wasn't it?

CHARMANE: It wasn't just that. Lisa and I have irrecognizable differences.

MISS ROSE: You mean irreconcilable differences.

CHARMANE: Oh. Well, anyway, we stopped being best friends the minute she said I looked like Bufford Simm's jersey cow in that dress.

MISS ROSE: What did you say back?

CHARMANE: I told Lisa that she looked quite fine in her dress . . . except it was an awful shame the way she sounded when she talked.

MISS ROSE: Now was that nice?

CHARMANE: Well, everybody knows she talks so fast it's like she's got a mouthful of stinging bees.

PEARL: I remember that dress, Charmane. Your mother showed it to me one time. It was orange chiffon with pink rosebuds, wasn't it?

CHARMANE: Yes, it was. I remember my date said my dress was just smashing. I thought he was insulting me till I found out he was talking British to me. *(Proudly)* Oh, it was a real glamorous dress, and straight out of the catalog too.

PEARL: Lisa must have been proud of her dress too.

CHARMANE: I suppose. *(Pause)* Now that I think about it, she did apologize to me the next day. *(Pause)* I guess I should have made plans to go to the wedding. Well, maybe I can send a little gift or something.

MISS ROSE: Yep. Bury the hatchet. That's what I always say. It's good for the body. Flushes out the toxins.

CHARMANE: Well, anyway, that wedding sure has been the talk of the town. That's for sure. They say it's the worst match of the century. I just hope Lisa knows what she's doing.

REBECCA *(with sudden interest):* Really? *(To* CHARMANE) Why do you say it's the worst match of the century? Actually, that's just what I was . . .

MISS ROSE: You know, you look so familiar to me, but I guess you're from out of town, so I don't know why you look familiar to me. Where are you from?

REBECCA: Dallas. *(Looks at her watch nervously)*

MISS ROSE: Do you have any relations living here?

REBECCA: Yes. *(Goes back to reading her magazine)*

MISS ROSE *(flustered):* You know, you look a lot like the Joneses. Are you any relation to them?

REBECCA *(puts down magazine, realizing there is no way to dodge* MISS ROSE'*s inquiries):* Yes, I am. I am Henry and Sara Jones' daughter.

MISS ROSE: Well, I swan. That makes you little Becky Jones. Why, I used to change your diapers when you came to visit down at the Baptist Church. Oh, and you used to do the cutest things when you were little. One time you and your mother were in Simpson's Grocery Store and you tore open all the caramel corn boxes from the bottom looking for all the prizes. And when somebody asked you where you learned to do that, you said, "That's the way Daddy always does it." Isn't that the cutest thing? *(Pause)* Imagine that . . . me *remembering* all that about you.

REBECCA *(smiles sourly to the side):* Yes, you've got quite a memory. *(Glances at her watch nervously)*

MISS ROSE: So what do you do in Dallas?

REBECCA: I'm an account executive for an advertising agency.

MISS ROSE: Oh, really? Well, I guess Henry and Sara are probably just glad to get you out of old Noley. There's not much here. If you'd stayed, you'd probably either be doing books for the hardware store or waiting on tables for a dollar an hour at the Paradise Café. (PEARL *clears her throat, trying to get* MISS ROSE'*s attention.* MISS ROSE *continues without noticing* PEARL.) The Paradise Café. It's a shame to say it, since I know the owners, but it is a disgrace to this town. (PEARL *clears her throat again and shakes her head at* MISS ROSE. MISS ROSE *continues without noticing.)* Yeah, the food there is pitiful . . . chews just like floor tile. And the coffee, ooh-wee, the coffee tastes just like it was brewed in an old spittoon. Why, just last year Sheriff Tyler found a big stinkbug floating in his stew. He was about to eat it, when he saw it heading for the side of the bowl. Of course, one can't tell you for sure about his story since the grocer saw Sheriff Tyler drinking something from a can while he was on duty. And I'll bet that wasn't sody pop he was drinking. *(Shaking her finger)* That should be a lesson to us all. We shouldn't be drinking sody pop out of a can, because at a distance people might think we're partaking of an intoxicating beverage. *(To* REBECCA*)* Well, anyway, as I was saying to you, Becky, you should be mighty thankful you didn't get stuck here working at the Paradise Café for the rest of your life. (PEARL *clears her throat even louder and again shakes her head at* MISS ROSE. MISS ROSE, *annoyed, answers to* PEARL.) Pearl, are you having some sinus trouble?

PEARL: No. *(Points to* CHARMANE *and mouths the words)* She works there!

MISS ROSE *(misunderstands* PEARL *and continues):* Charmane, you've been awful quiet. What do you think about the Paradise Café?

CHARMANE *(upset):* I don't know. I haven't *worked* there long enough to know.

MISS ROSE: Mercy me, I'm sorry, child. I guess I've really been talking out of turn. *(To* PEARL, *flustered)* Pearl, why didn't you stop me? (PEARL *shakes her head and sighs.)* Charmane, I thought you worked down at the bank. What happened, dear?

CHARMANE: Well, I did. But then they suddenly said they'd hired one too many people. I guess that *one* was me.

MISS ROSE: Isn't that just the way things go? *(Encouragingly)* I'll bet the coffee tastes better since you've been at the Paradise Café.

PEARL: Well, actually, I was there a couple of days ago, and you should have heard the customers brag on her. Charmane convinced them to change the menu and stop reusing the coffee grounds. It looked like business has really picked up. (PEARL *squirts perm solution on* CHARMANE*'s wave rods with plastic applicator bottle.)*

CHARMANE *(proudly):* It has. It's almost doubled. I even got a raise.

MISS ROSE: Well, if that isn't something. You're full of surprises. Just like the time you got married.

CHARMANE: What?

MISS ROSE: You surprised everybody because you said you were never meant to marry.

CHARMANE: Well, that was before I met Randall at Dempsey's Filling Station. There he was, pumping that gas and looking so intellectual.

MISS ROSE: Of course, *I* never married, as you all know. Once you set your eyes on higher things, those urges leave you. That's why I took up bird-watching. *(Pointing upward with her finger)* Look up, I always say. It refreshes the soul and softens our words. Marriage seems to do just the opposite. It clouds the spirit and sharpens the tongue. I know you agree with me, Pearl, because you never married.

PEARL *(kindly):* Now, Miss Rose, you know I've been engaged, and I was perfectly happy to marry.

MISS ROSE: Oh, yes, that's right. Bless your heart. Left at the altar. Isn't that just the way things go? You know, that man ought to be strung up on the nearest tree, and then horsewhipped.

REBECCA *(to* PEARL*)*: That must have been a hard time for you.

PEARL *(sincerely):* You're right. It wasn't the easiest of times, but I got over it, and I don't hold any grudges. *(Turns* CHARMANE *around and lowers the beauty chair)* OK. I'm finished here since Charmane is just getting a partial perm. Miss Rose said she didn't mind waiting, so Rebecca, you two can trade places.

REBECCA *(to* MISS ROSE*)*: Thanks. I really do appreciate this.

(CHARMANE *and* REBECCA *trade chairs.* PEARL *throws a plastic cape over* REBECCA *and begins to brush and section off her hair for hot rollers.)*

MISS ROSE: Oh, I don't mind. Don't you worry about me. I have some embroidery work to do here for my sister's birthday. (MISS ROSE *digs out a ghastly colored, odd-shaped pillow from her bag.)* I'm making it for her divan. *(Holds up the pillow for everyone to see)* Well, how do you like it?

(Brief silence)

CHARMANE *(with sour expression):* Isn't that pretty.

PEARL *(honestly):* I'm glad you've found a hobby that brings you so much pleasure.

MISS ROSE: I'm going to stitch all the Beatitudes right on the front. *(She reads the verse from the pillow, turning it sideways for the last two words.)* Right now I'm working on, "Blessed are the peacemakers: for they shall be called the children of God." I've got to hurry if she's to get this for her birthday. I was thinking about making some more of these pillows to sell. Since you like it so much, Charmane, maybe you'd like to be my first customer.

CHARMANE *(plastic smile):* Oh, well. Let me think on it.

REBECCA *(to* PEARL*)*: Maybe after we roll it, we could do something really special with my hair. You know some braids or long curls or something. I want to look perfect.

MISS ROSE *(to* REBECCA*)*: Well, you don't want to look too perfect. You should remember, good etiquette restrains one from outshining the bride.

REBECCA *(eyes lit with mischief):* I couldn't agree more. *(To* PEARL*)* You know, I came in your shop to get my hair fixed a couple of times when I was in high school.

PEARL: Yes, I think I remember. Your mother still comes in from time to time to get a permanent. She always talks about you. I know she's very proud of you.

REBECCA: Well, that's always good to hear.

PEARL: Do you enjoy your work in Dallas?

REBECCA: Yes, I do. It makes me very happy.

PEARL: That's a lot to be thankful for.

REBECCA: Yes, it is. Now all I need is someone to share all this happiness *with.* Actually, what I . . .

CHARMANE *(interrupting loudly):* Look out that picture window. Either Hank Dempsey's truck is belching smoke again, or that cloud has gotten as black as the bottom of a well.

MISS ROSE: Why that's a storm brewing over there. Oh, I love a good storm. *(Pause)* Mercy me! Did you see that? One of those big old tumbleweeds just flew straight across the window.

REBECCA: I heard on the car radio earlier that we're under a tornado watch.

CHARMANE *(anxiously):* Oh, really?

MISS ROSE *(leans forward as if to tell a secret):* Shhhhh. We'll have to listen very closely for the sound of the train. *(Quietly and mysteriously)* First, there will be a hush like death itself. It'll be so quiet and peaceful all around, you'll almost think the storm has passed . . . but then suddenly there it'll be. Boom!

(All jump.)

CHARMANE: What will it be? (MISS ROSE *looks a little confused.* CHARMANE *repeats* MISS ROSE'*s words to help her remember.)* You'll think the storm has passed, but then there it'll be. *(Anxiously)* What is it, Miss Rose?

MISS ROSE *(impatiently):* Why, the tornado, of course. It'll sound just like a locomotive tearing through your house.

REBECCA *(brightening):* I suppose they'll be forced to cancel the wedding because of this terrible weather, won't they?

MISS ROSE: In Noley? Never. Nothing stops anything in this town. Why, once I was attending a revival meeting up at the Methodist church, and we were singing "going to heaven" songs when Elston Dewberry's cattle got out. And let me tell you, those black Angus of his can get as feisty as his wife. Believe me, I know. Let's see, where was I? Oh yeah, anyway, all 200 of those bulky beasts came barreling across the wooden steps in front of the church. Well, it was the loudest thundering commotion you ever heard. We all thought it was the end, but we kept right on singing. So, come stampede or storm, they're bound to have that wedding. *(Leans forward to listen)* Shhhhh. Listen. Do you hear that?

CHARMANE: I wish you wouldn't do that. You're giving me the heebie-jeebies. *(After a pause, she lets out a high-pitched squeal.)* Oh no. I hear it too. I think it sounds like a . . . a train!

(Distant train sound)

REBECCA: OK, let's remain calm. We should all get down on the floor. (CHARMANE *and* REBECCA *get down on the floor.)* No, that's not right; we should all get in the bathtub. Or is it supposed to be in the closet? Pearl, what should we do? We have to do something, or we'll all be . . .

(CHARMANE *makes another high-pitched squeal, runs into the hall closet, and slams the door.* MISS ROSE *worriedly dabs her face and neck with her handkerchief, while the train sound continues to get louder.)*

REBECCA *(nervously):* Charmane is right. We'd better hurry. It seems to be coming this way. *(Heads toward closet)*

MISS ROSE *(heads toward the closet with* REBECCA *then turns back to* PEARL): Aren't you coming, Pearl?

PEARL *(looks at her watch and frowns):* You all go on. I have something to do first.

CHARMANE *(yells from the closet):* No! Pearl! Don't do it! Those are the people who always get killed in the movies!

PEARL *(calls back to* CHARMANE): I'll be there in just a minute.

(REBECCA *and* MISS ROSE *hurriedly join* CHARMANE *in the closet. The sound of the train continues to get louder.* PEARL *pulls a little stool over to the picture window and stands on it. She stretches her neck to see down the street and spots the railroad crossing lights flashing. She looks at her watch again, shakes her head, and chuckles.)*

CHARMANE *(yelling from closet):* Pearl, what are you doing out there?

(PEARL *walks over to the closet door.)*

MISS ROSE *(from closet):* For heaven's sake, Pearl, quit lollygagging, and get in here! Can't you hear that thing?

PEARL *(trying to hold back the laughter):* Well, I'm sure Great Plains Railroad would like to think they're as fast as a tornado.

(A moment of silence)

REBECCA: Did you say Great Plains? As in Railroad?

PEARL: Yep. That's the one. That silly train came an hour early today. I saw the lights flashing at the railroad crossing down the street.

CHARMANE: I feel just like a buffoon, as in animal at the zoo.

MISS ROSE: Charmane, you mean baboon!

CHARMANE: Oh. Say, what's that brushing against my ankle?

MISS ROSE *(nonchalantly):* Once I remember Pearl saying she had a problem with rats in her shop, but I've never noticed any real . . .

(MISS ROSE *is interrupted by the loud tumbling of boxes and general noise by* CHARMANE *and* REBECCA *trying to get out of the closet quickly.* REBECCA *and* CHARMANE *return to their chairs, trying to appear calm, while* PEARL *tries not to laugh.)*

CHARMANE *(to* PEARL*)*: What about my hair? This solution has been on my hair too long, hasn't it? I'm going to look like I've been put through a thrashing machine.

PEARL *(calmly):* Your hair is fine. *(To* MISS ROSE *in the closet)* Miss Rose? Are you all right?

MISS ROSE: Oh, yes. I'll be out directly. You know, I never knew a closet could be such a peaceful place. When I die, I want to be buried standing up in a closet.

CHARMANE *(lightheartedly sarcastic):* What a lovely sentiment, Miss Rose. But right now we've got to get this stuff washed off my hair.

REBECCA *(looking at her watch):* My word! I think I'm going to be late for my wedding. *(Quickly corrects herself)* I mean *the* wedding. It starts in just 30 minutes.

MISS ROSE *(comes out of the closet and looks at the time-piece fastened to her blouse):* Mercy. Just look at the time. I guess I do need to go ahead with my shampoo and set. I'm a *full* five minutes late for my grocery shopping.

CHARMANE *(panicking):* Pearl, don't leave me like this. I'll go home to Randall looking like a porcupine.

(PEARL *smiles imploringly at each of them with her hands on her hips.)*

MISS ROSE: Well, I guess my shopping can wait a little while.

PEARL: Thank you.

CHARMANE: I suppose I can rinse my hair myself in the sink. *(Lightly)* After all, out-of-town guests come before loyal patrons.

REBECCA: Thank you both, but I guess I've got something I need to confess. I'm not exactly in the wedding, per se.

CHARMANE *(to* MISS ROSE*)*: "Per se." I don't know French, but I have a feeling that means she got stuck handing out the rice bags after the ceremony. *(After a pause from* REBECCA*)* Not even the bags?

REBECCA: Actually, I wasn't even invited to the wedding.

MISS ROSE: Mercy me, child. Why would you want to drive all the way from Dallas to a wedding you're not even invited to. You seem to have more sense than that.

REBECCA: Maybe I don't. You see, I'm the former fiancée of the groom.

MISS ROSE *(puts her hand to her heart):* Well, I swan.

CHARMANE *(puzzled):* Why would you want to go to his wedding, if you don't mind my asking.

REBECCA: Well, let's just say I'm sure the bride and groom will be glad I didn't make it. *(Pause)* I'm really sorry I misled you all. I know it wasn't right. I'm not used to telling lies. It's just that I don't seem to be myself lately.

MISS ROSE: You still love him, don't you, dear?

REBECCA: Yes, I do . . . although I don't know why. He's got an Achilles' heel.

CHARMANE *(encouragingly):* You know, I think I had that one time, but Dr. Purvis fixed me right up. He said all I needed was better arch support.

REBECCA: What I'm trying to say is, he has trouble making up his mind. One time he actually went back into his apartment three times to change the color of his socks for a job interview. He said if clothes make the man, then he couldn't afford to make any stupid mistakes. Right, I said, but didn't you just miss your plane to your job interview?

CHARMANE: He doesn't sound that bad to me. Randall never even owned three pair of socks.

REBECCA: Maybe it really isn't important. Maybe all that matters is that I love him. Only now he wants to marry someone else. *(Pause)* It's funny. All my life I've believed there's a purpose for everything. That if you loved God, everything would work for good. Right now, I'm having a really hard time with those words.

PEARL *(gently squeezes* REBECCA*'s shoulder from behind):* I've known that feeling too.

REBECCA: You have?

PEARL: After I was left standing there at the church on my wedding day, it was just like a dark winter had settled in on my spirit. I was beginning to wonder if there'd ever been such a thing as spring. I'd lost sight of those words too.

REBECCA: What happened?

PEARL: Well, as time went by, I learned some things about that gentleman I hadn't known. It dawned on me that the loss had really been God's mercy. He hadn't failed me. It had been the other way around.

(CHARMANE, *tearful over the conversation, blows her nose loudly. Attention is suddenly on* CHARMANE. *Embarrassed over her emotions, she quickly fans the air with her hand.)*

CHARMANE: Pearl, I think the ammonia in this perm is bothering my eyes. I'm going to rinse if it's all right.

REBECCA: Please, go ahead, Pearl, if you need to rinse Charmane. I'd like to just sit here for a minute.

PEARL *(to* REBECCA): You go right ahead. *(Looks at the timer, shuts it off, and then turns to* CHARMANE) The timer was just about to go off. We'll rinse and then put the neutralizer on.

(PEARL *goes over to the rinsing chair with* CHARMANE. PEARL *rinses* CHARMANE'S *hair and then squirts neutralizer on from an applicator bottle.* REBECCA *is unrolling her hair slowly.)*

MISS ROSE *(to* REBECCA): Maybe you'd like some tea. I've kept a tea bag here in my purse for years just for emergencies. Tea always makes me feel strong as an ox and fit as a fiddle.

REBECCA *(smiling):* I guess I'll pass. Thanks anyway.

MISS ROSE: Where will you go now, dear? Will you stay with your parents out at the farm for a while, or go back to Dallas?

REBECCA: I think I'll head back to Dallas. I could use some time alone to think.

MISS ROSE: Yes.

REBECCA: PEARL, what do I owe you?

PEARL: My goodness. Don't you dare get your money out.

REBECCA: Thanks.

MISS ROSE *(moves downstage to look out picture window):* It looks like the storm has passed us by. *(Sounding disappointed)* And I was sure it was brewing up a real ornery one. It just goes to show you, you never really know how things are going to turn out. *(To* REBECCA) At least you'll have some good driving weather going back to Dallas. *(Steps closer to window for a better look outside)* Mercy me. Will you just look at that. Girls, come over and look at this. It's a double rainbow. Why, I haven't seen one of those in a blue moon.

(PEARL, CHARMANE, *and* REBECCA *join* MISS ROSE *at the picture window. They all stare at the rainbow in awe.)*

REBECCA: Oh, it is pretty, isn't it?

CHARMANE: It reminds me of the giant lollipop Randall bought me at the state fair last year.

MISS ROSE: I think that's the grandest one I've ever seen.

PEARL: You know, when I was a little girl, I liked to think that rainbows came when the angels painted God's house. I used to imagine them spilling a little from their pails on purpose, just to show us how lovely heaven would be.

MISS ROSE: It *is* just like a piece of heaven . . . so perfect and peaceful.

(Pause)

REBECCA: Well, I guess I'd better be going.

PEARL: Please don't feel like you have to go. Maybe you'd like to stay a while longer to get your bearings.

REBECCA: Thanks a lot, Pearl, but I'd better go. *(Smiling)* I won't be getting my bearings back for a long time anyway. *(Picks up her purse)* Thank you all for your understanding. *(Looks down at* MISS ROSE'S *pillow)* I hope you get your pillow finished for your sister's birthday.

MISS ROSE *(being cheerful for* REBECCA): Lord willing, and the creek don't rise.

REBECCA *(to* CHARMANE): Oh, and good luck at the Paradise Café. Sounds like you're doing a great job. Maybe someday when I'm back in town, I'll drop by.

CHARMANE: Sure. I'll even buy you a cup of coffee.

(REBECCA *smiles at each of them, walks toward the door, and then turns back around.)*

PEARL: Let us hear from you. Come by the shop here or the house anytime. You're always welcome.

REBECCA: I really appreciate that. Well, you all take care.

(PEARL, MISS ROSE, *and* CHARMANE *continue to center their attention on* REBECCA.)

MISS ROSE: You take care too. And watch out for the sheriff's pet peacocks when you're driving out of town. Those stupid birds think they're a pack of dogs . . . always chasing cars. So be careful.

REBECCA *(smiling):* I will. Bye now.

PEARL: Bye-bye, dear.

MISS ROSE: Bye.

CHARMANE *(waves):* Bye.

(All stand and watch as REBECCA *opens the shop door to leave.* MATTHEW *enters the shop at the same time* REBECCA *is leaving. He nearly knocks her off her feet.)*

MATTHEW: Oh, excuse me, ma'am! I'm really sorry. *(He turns and sees the other women.)* Hello, ladies.

(Because the attention is still focused on REBECCA, *they all greet* MATTHEW *absently.)*

PEARL: Rebecca, this is Matthew Stevens. Matthew, Rebecca Jones.

MATTHEW: Glad to meet you. I'm sure sorry about the door. Hope you're all right.

REBECCA: I'm fine. And I'm glad to meet you too.

MATTHEW *(to* PEARL, *sincerely):* Well, anyway, I promised the preacher I'd go around and remind everybody about the potluck tonight down at the Baptist Church. Actually, it's the First Annual Noley Flag Day Potluck Supper and Extravaganza.

MISS ROSE: Whew! That's a mouthful.

MATTHEW: Yeah, I know it. At first they were going to just call it the Flag Day Potluck, but they said that sounded too boring, so there you go. Anyway, the Gurney family is going to play some patriotic songs on their kazoos . . . and let's see, oh yeah, and the Gurneys donated the prize for the free drawing too.

MISS ROSE *(unexcited):* Yeah, I heard about the prize . . . free kazoo lessons for a whole year.

(Pause)

MATTHEW *(romantically):* Pearl, I was hoping you could still go with me tonight.

PEARL: Wouldn't miss it for the world!

(The other women exchange happy grins over the romantic interaction between MATTHEW *and* PEARL.*)*

MATTHEW: Oh, and, of course, I hope *all* you ladies can make it tonight.

MISS ROSE: Well, I would, but I've got to get busy and finish this pillow for my sister's birthday. *(Holds up pillow for* MATTHEW *to see)* How do you like it?

MATTHEW *(pauses with odd expression, trying to think of something good to say about the pillow):* Well, you must love her a whole lot to go to so much trouble.

CHARMANE: I suppose Randall and I could go. We're not Baptists, but since it's their first annual one and everything. I could even bring some of my stuffed livers with my famous prune-mustard sauce.

(To the side, MISS ROSE *pats her chest and clears her throat at the mention of* CHARMANE'S *unappetizing dish.)*

REBECCA *(suddenly realizing that the attention is on her for a response to the invitation):* It sounds like a nice evening, but I'm on my way back to Dallas. Thanks for the invitation, though.

MATTHEW: Certainly is a lot of coming and going today. Just like that wedding at the church today. Too bad, wasn't it?

MISS ROSE *(loudly):* Too bad about what?

CHARMANE: What do you mean?

REBECCA *(anxiously):* What happened?

MATTHEW: Well, they didn't have it. The wedding was called off.

PEARL *(calmly, but concerned):* What happened, Matthew?

MATTHEW: Well . . .

MISS ROSE *(loudly, happy for the chance that it might help* REBECCA*):* Yes, goodness gracious! Tell us what happened. Did he stand her up? Did she stand him up? For heaven's sake, Mr. Stevens, why don't you tell us what happened?

MATTHEW *(calmly):* Well, they both stood each other up. Never saw the likes of it before. First, the best man came in and said that the groom wasn't coming because he was in love with somebody else. Well, that put the bride's family in a real spitting mood, until the bride's maid of honor arrived saying that the bride wasn't coming because she didn't really love him. Well, as soon as all that soaked in, the parents said it was a shame to waste all that good cake and punch, so we helped ourselves to . . .

REBECCA: Excuse me. Did the groom mention the woman's name? Who he was in love with?

MATTHEW: Well, not in front of everyone, but I'm pretty good friends with the best man, so he told me off to the side. I think it was . . .

REBECCA: Rebecca?

MATTHEW: Yeah, that's it. Say, how did you know . . .

REBECCA: Oh, Mr. Stevens! *(In her excitement kisses* MATTHEW *full on the mouth)* You've just made me a very happy woman. In fact, I'm so happy I think I feel guilty.

(MATTHEW *is surprised and confused, but glad for* REBECCA.)

MISS ROSE: Isn't that just the way things go?

CHARMANE *(clasping her hands together and giggling):* Oh, I knew it. I knew it all along.

PEARL *(genuinely):* We're all so happy for you.

REBECCA: Oh, Pearl. *(She hugs* PEARL.)

MATTHEW *(suddenly understanding):* You mean, you're *the* Rebecca? Well, what do you know! Congratulations!

REBECCA *(suddenly a little confused):* Wait a minute.

CHARMANE: What is it? What's the matter?

REBECCA: Something's not quite right here. I haven't been looking at this from every angle. I think I smell a rat. (CHARMANE *glances around the room wor-*

riedly.) Don't you see? He did it again. He can't make up his mind. How can I marry a man who keeps flip-flopping like that . . . especially about marriage?

MISS ROSE: Isn't that just the way things go? First, you don't have him, and you can't live without him. Now you have him, and he's bound to make your life miserable. It's a good thing I'm not the fainting type, 'cause this could make a body dizzy.

REBECCA: I know it seems crazy. I don't want to feel this way. I do love him, but . . . oh, Pearl, what am I going to do?

PEARL: I guess spending some time on your knees is the best answer right now.

REBECCA: It just doesn't sound like the easiest answer. But I know you're right. *(Shakes her head, smiling, still a little bewildered)* What a decision.

PEARL: Listen, when you start to feel low from wondering what's going to happen to you, just remember that God has you in the palm of His hand, and nothing can separate you from that love. You're going to be just fine. I know it.

REBECCA: Somehow I believe you. It's funny. Now I know why my mother always says, "That Pearl, she's as good with hearts as she is with hair." *(Hugs* PEARL. *Everyone chuckles heartily.* REBECCA *gently pulls away and asks warmly)* And what about you, Pearl? Did everything work out for you? Are you happy?

PEARL: Oh, yes. (PEARL *and* MATTHEW *look at each other lovingly.)* I have as much joy as my heart can hold.

MISS ROSE: Isn't that just the way things go?

(All chuckle with MISS ROSE.)

(Blackout)

PERFORMANCE LICENSING AGREEMENT

Lillenas Drama Resources
Performance Licensing
P.O. Box 419527, Kansas City, MO 64141

Name ______________________________

Organization ______________________________

Address ______________________________

City ______________________ State __________ Zip __________

Play ______________________________

Number of performances intended ______________________________

Approximate dates ______________________________

Amount remitted* $ ______________________________

Mail to Lillenas at the address above

Order performance copies of this script from your local bookstore or directly from the publisher.

*Each script: $15.00 for the first performance; $10.00 for each subsequent performance.